Gaia's Own

Gaia's Own

Every Child's Guide To
Living In Harmony With Nature

Dharshana Bajaj

Gaia's Own: Every Child's Guide To Living In Harmony With Nature

Deepest gratitude for the Early **Readers' Reviews** for
*Gaia's Own: Every Child's Guide To Living In
Harmony With Nature*

"A model of the kind of optimistic and caring conversations we need more of!" ~ ***Bill McKibben*, environmentalist and author, *We Are Better Together***

"We appreciate it very much ... It conveys the kind of spirit shared by many Greenpeace supporters." ~ **Greenpeace International**

"Dharshana has created a sensitive and timely book that not only introduces young people to the urgent environmental questions of the day, but also opens up the conversation in a way that allows them to make their own decisions and discoveries. Beautifully put together." ~ ***Parvathi Naya*r, artist and writer who works with water, space, and urban memory**

"This is an educational, thorough and entertaining read that will guide every child and teenager toward an existence of love and health. It will encourage them to get creative as well, to respond to the challenges they will be facing throughout their lives.

"I highly recommend Gaia's Own: Every Child's Guide to Living in Harmony with Nature to educators and parents." ~ ***Julia Hones*, writer and poet**

"It's a good book." ~ ***Maneka Sanjay Gandhi*, politician and activist**

"Like healthy food, this book feels like a must include in the diet of every child's library!" ~ **Amazon Reader**

This book is dedicated to my parents, and my son —like your name may you be Radiant always

Contents

Foreword

It is profoundly humbling for me to write these few words of the Foreword to this book for children.

As a child coming from a low income family, I remember the joy of climbing trees filled with fruits, birds chirping, wild flowers bursting into splendor of colors befriended by lovely butterflies, flying insects and other creatures of different shapes and vigor.

That garden city is choked today, and so are its children – with multiple problems, including breathing and infected lungs.

A slow but affirmative action by citizens is happening by awakened citizens – mothers, uncles, and children themselves.

As the popular saying by Lester Brown goes – we have not inherited this beautiful Earth from our forefathers; we have borrowed it from our children. And it is time that we honor that debt by returning it in the way it was given to us or at least improve it a bit for having used it.

As a child I also remember my dear mother pressing a soft old dampened cotton saree to my forehead whenever I was down with high fever as she could not take me to a doctor soon enough. She knew it was fatal to allow the temperature of my body to go up anymore.

Now Mother Earth is raging with a fever that is consuming her and therefore all of us. Every part of her – mountains, trees, flowers, animals, rivers, oceans, and even deserts – are crumbling and gasping to sustain life.

Children and young adults across the world are realizing this and taking leadership.

This is a wonderful book – timely, thoughtful, warmly informing, and enabling the awareness of the critical interdependence of human existence and the natural world.

I know this from my walks across the world.

I also know that the global warming and climate change impact first, worst, and hardest the most vulnerable people, who have contributed least to the problems.

During my first walk to Copenhagen from Oxford, in 2009, I carried a backpack weighing approximately 20 kilos – the weight of fire wood and water that young 11-year-old Judith carried to help her mother and in so doing she was unable to attend school. I carried her story to illustrate the differential impact of climate change.

As I am writing this Foreword – Spain is raging with fire and little beautiful Britain is burning with a historically high temperature.

Cloud bursts, landslides, and floods are ravaging our own India – and destroying lives and livelihoods and emasculating our rich biodiversity of the Western Ghats as I witnessed, including the conflict between Man and Beast – with the glorious elephants going amok due to less food being available for them and the ancient elephant tracks being encroached upon by various so-called development projects. This battle will only grow fiercer unless we act – NOW.

This urgency, of addressing the issues right now, needs to be acknowledged and this book portrays the need for that urgency.

I congratulate the author Dharshana, for the passionate, thoughtful, critical, and compassionate book. I shall carry it for my next walk in Madurai in September 2022 – talking about developing a non-violent economy – and soon again as I walk in my second spiritual home – Africa.

I would also like to add that this book is not for children alone, but it is an essential must-read for every adult – because it is our duty to protect this planet.

Pushpanath Krishnamurthy
Global Consultant, Climate Change Campaigner, Trainer,
Mentor, Speaker

Preface

There are already several books on the environment out there. Why one more? What is so different about this book that every child should read it? Or anyone for that matter?

This book shares concerns about the current environmental issues plaguing Earth, yes. It also shares information on what is being done to alleviate these problems as well as fresh perspectives on what needs to be done further to completely course-correct and help maintain the balance in Nature conducive to a harmonious existence.

Is that possible at all, one may skeptically wonder. This book shows us it can be done.

Gaia's Own: Every Child's Guide To Living In Harmony With Nature is an invitation to every child to get back to the fold, bringing all of humanity with them. Gaia, Mother Earth, is calling. She is calling all her sons and daughters back. It's time for each of us to rise to the occasion, reset priorities, and follow the way home.

This book brings to your attention not only facts, but also insights of the wise, both ancient and contemporary, on the radical, deep, and sometimes even simple changes that are required of us. So simple as to be child's play. And that is why this book is for children everywhere, and the little child in all of us. For we are all Gaia's own.

Man belongs to Earth, Earth does not belong to man. ~ *Native American Proverb.*

In every walk with nature one receives far more than he seeks. ~ *John Muir*

Climate change is the single biggest thing that humans have ever done on this planet. The one thing that needs to be bigger is our movement to stop it. ~ *Bill McKibben*

Chapter 1: Gaia's Own

Hi Nana,

Hope your flight was fun. I'm so sorry I missed saying goodbye yesterday. One bear hug due :)

The first day of our new school year today was great. It was good to see Ashu, Naina, and everyone again after the summer vacations. Can't say the same thing about Avi though! Or Jia! Some things just don't change! We all had a pleasant surprise waiting for us in school though. A new principal! Actually, that was what made this a fabulous day back.

Anne Ma'am, our new princi, has radically altered our curriculum. We had our first Earth Hour today, and I'm so proud of it already! So, the new deal is that this academic year, our 7th grade and the senior classes are to have one class every day dedicated to the *environment*. It's an amazing program which I'm sure you'll approve of. Today was just the introductory session where they explained the schedule to us, and it really sounds great. I hope they pull it off to the 'T'! Can you imagine, one whole hour every day to be spent looking at, talking about, and thinking of our place in Nature? At first, it sounded very boring, but once Anne Ma'am started her presentation, all of us were spellbound.

Of course, we've all heard of it before, that *climate change* is underway, bringing about some very drastic, unpleasant consequences. We have all seen *Greta Thunberg*'s speech on

YouTube, participated in the ban on *plastics* imposed a while ago, and read about it in our school books to know that there is some kind of a problem out there. But I for one had no idea that we are in the midst of an urgent, and the biggest, problem facing humanity! Anne Ma'am said over the past several years we humans have been using up Earth's resources indiscriminately. Human actions, like *deforestation* for agriculture and *industrialization*, are changing the climate in unexpected ways that are destroying Nature. For instance, did you know that in May of 2020 there had been a massive oil spill in Russia which forever changed the lives of thousands of people?

Apparently, a fuel tank at a power plant in Siberia collapsed when the supports holding it up were dislodged due to the melting *permafrost* beneath. Nearly 20,000 tons of diesel fuel spilled into the nearby rivers, the Ambarnaya and the Daldykan rivers, as well as a local water reservoir. The damage to the environment was extensive and the President, Vladimir Putin, even declared a state of emergency. Anne Ma'am showed us pictures of how dangerous chemicals from the diesel fuel had dissolved in the water, killing several fish, birds, and animals.

So, to sum it up, it appears that mankind has dug itself into a pit, and now we (us kids?) have to find ways to climb back out! The solution Anne Ma'am has come up with is the Earth Hour. From this year on, all classes in the secondary school will have one hour every day of the week dedicated to discussions, presentations, guest lectures, and time out in Nature. She said this was to make each one of us more aware of all the issues involved so that when it is our turn to be "grownups" we can make wiser decisions to save the planet!

Seriously! I mean, sure, I love the idea of being a "superhero," but what can we do? We are just kids, right? Isn't this something the authorities should worry about? Those who can do something about it, like the government, scientists, and other experts? How can ordinary people like you and me stop climate change or solve the problem? Actually Nana, right now as I look out of the window, everything seems fine, normal, perfectly alright! Makes me wonder, is there really a climate problem?

Anyway, my first presentation for Earth Hour is to be made next week. Mama told me to check with you about what would be an interesting and appropriate topic. She said you would have a better idea as you deal with this already. What do you think I should talk about? Please suggest something that's inspiring, and fun! And that requires no mind-numbing statistics, OK?

When do you get back from Brazil? Stay safe and don't be eaten by the anacondas!

Much love,
Satvika

My dearest Satvi,

Hearty congratulations to your new Anne Ma'am! I love the sound of this Earth Hour. Well done! Knowledge is power as they say, and the better informed you are, the more effective you can be.

Is there a climate problem? In the last 4.5 billion years of Earth's history, there have been many changes in it. Now you study that we have seven continents and five oceans, but millions of years ago, there was just one large supercontinent on Earth, which we call *Pangea*. Because of various forces, like wind and the movement of the Earth's *tectonic plates* way beneath the surface, the planet has transformed to what it is today. If one were to go further back in time, scientists believe the origin of

Earth, as of the rest of our solar system and the universe, was a single point, a dot, which expanded, ballooned, grew so large that it then exploded, in a *Big Bang*, to become this universe we know today. And the universe continues to expand now. So, change is the essence of our universe, and of our lives.

Over the billions of years of Earth's history, the climate has changed a lot, too. Usually these changes occur gradually over several years, even centuries. Remember the movie *Ice Age*? On a day-to-day basis, we cannot observe these changes. But the rise in overall temperatures in the last two centuries, ever since industrialization, has occurred at an alarmingly fast rate. Mankind has made some amazing discoveries and inventions, like electricity, motorized vehicles, and airplanes. This "progress" has changed our lives completely, bringing lots of conveniences to us. But in the process, we have also changed the natural world in ways that had never been anticipated. In our march to greater comfort, success, and glory, we have blindly trampled over all other creatures and life forms along our way. Our unabated passions not only led to more and more of coal and oil being burned to create more energy, we've ended up burning holes in the very atmosphere that protects us, in the ozone layer, forever changing its composition!

This man-made, or *anthropogenic*, unnatural climate change is what we are dealing with now. It has been causing all sorts of unexpected events, "natural disasters," affecting all life forms on Earth, endangering our very existence. But how dire is the situation? Of course, the experts know more than we lay people do. They say if we don't change our ways, in a hundred years, this whole planet will be a desert or a dry, dead land. But scientists cannot be 100% sure of their estimations and predictions. Their analyses and warnings of impending threats are based on models and assumptions. There is no accurate data they can use, though they have compelling arguments. However, whether there is really any impending threat or if the changes are all part of the natural process, I see this scenario as an invitation for all of us, yes, ordinary citizens like me and even children like you, to reestablish our lost connection with Nature. That, I believe, is the root cause of a lot of problems today.

Do you know Satvi, the *Native American* tribes had lived for thousands of years off the land. Like all the ancient tribes across the world, they had a strong connection with the world around them. When a child turned 12, about your age, they were sent to spend time alone in Nature! The young boys and girls would sleep in the trees, far away from others, wait there for days if required, until they had that special "dream," which the Native Americans believed revealed a personal message from the universal spirit about their life and future. The Native Americans believed that this universal force, which they called The Great Spirit or *Wakan Tanka,* has its way, or rhythm, and "When you lose the rhythm of the drumbeat of God, you are lost from the peace and rhythm of life."

The ancient peoples everywhere understood the importance of Nature. The Chinese called the way of the universe The Tao, and the Greeks called her Gaia, or Mother Earth, the bountiful one, full of unconditional love. And it's not just our ancestors. Several people even today vouch for this interrelationship between all things in our universe. In 1970, two scientists, James Lovelock and Lynn Margulis, put forward the *Gaia Theory,* which states that this entire planet is one living organism.

Earth is not just a large rock spinning around the Sun. It is a living system, and we are a part of it. However, now we have become estranged from this "system." Most of our problems have arisen because mankind has been taking decisions from this position of disconnection, by following the mind instead of the heart. Therefore, now a basic reset is called for, a shift in consciousness from seeing one's self as being just "li'l ol' me" to what one truly is – a unique and significant part of this living, breathing organism called Earth.

So let the scientists and leaders do whatever they are apt to do, believe me, each one is doing their best (mostly) with regards to this problem, based on their own understanding of it. And let us all do our bit as well. For just as our actions in the past have created some unexpected, unpleasant circumstances, hurting the system and our fellow creatures, what we choose to do now and in the future can help fix or heal this planet we call home. It is time for the rest of us to step up and do what we are led to do from within, by our "inner voice."

Yes Satvika, like your principal has been led to initiate this program for you. She obviously is ahead of a lot of others and seems intuitively guided. Do you know what intuition is, Satvika? If you don't already know, you soon will when you start spending more time in Nature. That is the most important step to healing our relationship with Mother Earth and the Great Spirit. Spend more time in Nature, listen, and observe things in silence. You will be amazed at how insights present themselves to you. The more you allow yourself to be led by these insights, the stronger your intuition and instinct become.

As a matter of fact, that is exactly the topic I recommend for your first presentation for Earth Hour. Why it is more important to spend some time every day in Nature, and to just be. I've always thought these modern times are too biased toward action. People are always in a hurry, chasing some goal. I know, you children, too, are always busy, spend your days shuttling from school to class after class. With very little time spent outdoors or to yourself. You have no idea what you are all missing! That is what has to change, where we place our values!

Spending time in Nature is one of the best things you can do for yourself. No matter where I am in the world, or my concerns at the moment, the minute I step out for my daily walk my worries just vanish into thin air. Suddenly I'm fully in the present. Walking then becomes a form of meditation. It allows one to just be. To listen to what the universe has to say. For as the Native

Americans well knew, when you stay still long enough, the Earth speaks to you.

We modern folks have lost that appreciation for Nature, for this planet. And that truly has been our loss.

Now I'm not suggesting you should go alone and sleep in some tree! My point is that to truly value something, you have to pay attention to it. So, go spend time outside, pay attention to the natural world. You have to develop a feel for Nature, learn to love it more, and that cannot happen by spending your time indoors or watching endless TV.

It all comes down to how we choose to see things, and how grounded we are, how connected with our own souls and intuition. This reminds me of that time, when your mom, our first child, was just born. As an anxious first-time father, I asked your Nani, "Why don't babies come with manuals!?" Your amused Nani replied wisely, "We all come with our personal manuals, Yogi. That's what they call 'instinct'."

Spending more time outdoors not only helps us be more calm and grounded, it helps us listen to our "instincts." And when we start following our instincts, life just seems to flow beautifully, because one is then aligned with what Life itself, what Gaia, wants for us as well.

So, go ahead and enlighten your class on Gaia. Tell your friends what they have been missing by not spending enough time out on their terrace or parks, listening to the birds, watching the sunrise, feeling the energy of Mother Earth all around. Better yet, take them outdoors! Go, "hang out" with Nature!

All the best with your presentation, Satvika. I'll be back in Chennai in a fortnight, in time for your birthday. The anacondas are not the problem here in this part of the rainforest. But the mosquitoes! They are another thing altogether!

Which reminds me of that line by the Dalai Lama, "If you think you are too small to make a difference, try sleeping with a mosquito!"

Hugs,
Yogesh

Gateway To Gaia: No.1
Spend Time In Nature

"In clinical studies, we have proven that 2 hours of nature sounds a day significantly reduces stress hormones up to 800% and activates 500–600 DNA segments known to be responsible for healing and repairing the body." ~ *Dr. Joe Dispenza*

1) Start spending as much time as possible out of doors every day, in your garden, terrace, or the park near your home.

2) Go on treks with your family when you get the chance. Travel and explore the many wonders of Nature that we are all blessed with.

3) Starting this week, journal your experiences, thoughts, and feelings when you are out and about. Was there any new bird you spotted? A new flower? How did it feel to have the wind ruffle your hair? Did you feel energized?

4) How many parks are there in your city or town? How many have you visited? Visit at least one this week.

5) What other geographical features define your city or town of residence? If there is a beach nearby, when was the last time you visited? Take your family there.

6) How do you think this compares to 2 hours of screen time watching a movie? Which do you think is crucial to your well-being?

7) In some of your daily walks, identify spots where you can plant seeds, and then go back there to plant seeds of fruits you've eaten. If you can water this place, do so the next time you are there. If you must get anyone's permission to do this, like a caretaker may be, please ask first. Chances are they'd be delighted to have you help.

8) Find a leaf or flower you like, and keep it inside this book, on this page. See how it changes over a period of time. Find out the name of that leaf or flower.

The greatest error of a man is to think that he is weak by nature, evil by nature. Every man is divine and strong in his real nature. What are weak and evil are his habits, his desires, and thoughts, but not himself. ~ *Ramana Maharshi*

As for those who would take the whole world to tinker it as they see fit, I observe that they never succeed: for the world is a sacred vessel not made to be altered by man…So the wise man discards extreme inclinations to make sweeping judgments or to live a life of excess. ~ *Lao Tzu*

To meditate means to go home to yourself. Then you know how to take care of the things that are happening inside you, and you know how to take care of the things that happen around you. ~ *Thich Nhat Hanh*

Chapter 2: Meditation

Hi Nana,

Thank you for the lovely gift again. Surprised to note the similarities between the *Harry Potter* books and *The Lord of The Rings*. And thank you so much for being here on my birthday! I wish you could have joined us for the weekend at Radisson Blue as well. Nicky and I swam for hours, and even Nani came into the pool for some time. It was great cycling around those huge gardens far from the city. You are right, spending time in Nature is its own kind of fun. I even spotted a kingfisher!

We've been having some very interesting sessions of Earth Hour this week. I wanted to share some of it with you. Some very shocking facts have been presented to make the whole class sit up. Why don't people talk about all of this more? Papa says the information appears as small news items in the daily newspaper. Why isn't there more coverage? Just because it doesn't happen under their noses, people don't care? Or is it that too many things are happening that are not OK, so no one is shocked anymore?

Nadia made her presentation today, on the fires raging in Brazil. It disturbed me more than the others knowing you had been there recently. How come you never mentioned them, Nana? Did you see any of those sites? I mean, sure, we know deforestation happens so we can have more land for agriculture, etc., and that it is one of the causes of forest fires. But what is with the numbers? Nadia said thousands of forest fires break out in the Amazon Rainforest every year destroying large portions of it. As per BBC, in the first seven months of 2020, more than 13,000 sq km (5,019 sq miles or more than ten times the size of Chennai!) of the Brazilian Amazon was burned. This was according to the analysis of satellite data provided by a Dr. Michelle Kalamandeen, a tropical ecologist, on the Amazon rainforest. Do you know her?

Nadia also said while some of these forest fires, especially the ones in summer, occur due to natural causes, most of them are man-made! She said if deforestation in the Amazon rainforest continues at the current scale, the forest will no longer be able to produce enough moisture, and will eventually transform into a dry savanna. This will have a domino effect, decimating the plants, animals, birds, insects, trees, and other life forms, that is, the *biodiversity*, in the rainforest, and also altering the global water cycle. What is the global water cycle, though? I didn't get that part of it. But it does not sound like something we should be happy about!

How can the Brazilians do this to their own country, to the beautiful rainforest? The tribal people there, the Muras, are very unhappy about the situation. The French President Emmanuel Macron also tweeted, "Our house is burning. Literally. The Amazon – the lungs which produce 20% of our planet's oxygen – is on fire."

How did we get here Nana? I mean, how did mankind come to this point? Why didn't we see it coming? And yet, my garden is quiet and peaceful, and all seems well in my world! Feeling very blessed indeed.

When you were here this time Nana, you said during my time spent in Nature I should also try meditating. I tried it yesterday. I sat on a terrace bench like Buddha, with my eyes closed. Could barely sit still for a few minutes! How do you do it for hours? How did Buddha and that 5-year-old Dhruv do it for days on end? Mind-boggling!

Take care, Nana. I'm missing those days before Earth Hour and all the knowledge we are being exposed to now. Ignorance truly was blissful! Suddenly it seems like life is a serious affair, and we cannot make choices as carelessly as before.

Anyways, I've decided to make my next month's presentation on water. Listening about the fire problems in Brazil, I was reminded of the flood we had in Chennai a few years ago. My first and (thankfully) only personal experience of climate change-related disasters! Is there anything about water that is special that you would like me to include in my talk?

Miss you much!
Satvika

My dearest Satvika,

"Forewarned is forearmed" — do you recall that line from the classic *Treasure Island*? Consider your Earth Hour and any information you receive on our environment as part of the education that prepares you and your generation for the future. Ideally, we should not have come to this. But when our species began first exploiting Nature for its survival, using its one great strength, its intelligence, to develop activities like agriculture and later industries, the impact on the environment was never anticipated. No one has wanted this willfully, of course. But human errors due to bad judgment and a selfish focus have created this mess. When we thus collectively reframe our focus and goals in life, when we adopt ways of being and habits that enhance our own well-being as well as that of the Earth, things are bound to change in the other direction. That's Newton's 3rd Law, right? Every action has an equal and opposite reaction!

Of course, there are certain disasters that happen suddenly, destroying lives and livelihoods. Like the explosion of the nuclear factory in Chernobyl in 1984. That was a man-made error that impacted the natural surroundings and the biodiversity there with its radioactive emissions. In less than 48 hours people living nearby had to be evacuated, to rebuild their lives elsewhere. Much like the politically induced disastrous events like the India and Pakistan partition.

Climatic changes, on the other hand, occur silently, over several decades or even centuries. The carbon and other harmful gases put out by the actions of previous generations of humanity, unknowingly, have changed the climate for us in the present and the immediate future. Some of those changes cannot be corrected completely, so we are finding ways to adapt to them, like we adapt to the increase in temperature and sudden rainfalls, etc. Now there is greater awareness among people that our actions can have adverse consequences, so more and more people are waking up and contributing to finding ways of living that are more in tune with Nature.

There are several organizations around the world, like WWF and Greenpeace, formed purely by concerned citizens, or activists as they are also called. These groups spread awareness among the too-busy-to-care laymen as well as question the decisions of leaders of state and commerce when they seem ignorant or uncaring of how they are contributing to the climate crisis.

Politically as well, more and more leaders are becoming aware and concerned, like President Macron, and are striving to help humanity correct its past ways. Many summits and conferences have been held in the past decades to arrive at a consensus on what needs to be done. The leaders are signing agreements, like the Paris Agreement, and passing new laws. But all of that is only symptomatic correction. That is not enough. Radical change, from the bottom-up, involving each one of us is called for. Because the Earth and its well-being affect us all equally. We are all children of Gaia, and each of our actions and our disparate ways of thinking contribute toward the change. Each one of us can, and should, strive to make a difference. Just start with what you can. Baby steps are good. Spend more time in Nature. Its wonders will have you fall in love with it all in no time. You will see what a treasure we have been blessed with.

And yes, meditation, or just being, still and silent, is very, very important. Who was it that said, "a busy mind is no mind at all"?

Meditation is one of the crucial ways to get in touch with your inner voice, your intuition. That is your direct link to the universal spirit, to Gaia. That's like your dynamic manual for living that is constantly being updated. As a wildlife photographer for many years, though I am very familiar with all sorts of cameras, anytime we have to upgrade to the latest technology, I find I'm helpless without the accompanying manual! And we humans are so much more complex than cameras, right? How can we operate sanely, optimally, and effectively when we are cut off from our intuition? Not possible, my dear. That is precisely how we've collectively landed in this ecological soup! By overriding our intuition, by ignoring our instincts.

The only way we can swim out of this soup is to first center ourselves. That begins with not doing things, but "being." By that, I mean being mindful of your breath, of your body, and bringing yourself completely to the present moment, without any thoughts of the future or the past. That is meditation. Yes, we can do it Buddha's way, sitting under a tree, far away in a forest, away from all distractions. But any act done with mindfulness is also a type of meditation. When you are on your terrace, you could walk more mindfully, paying attention to all things around you, instead of listening to music or thinking about other things. That then becomes a walking meditation. Easy? Yes, it is. Likewise, when you eat your meals, do so mindfully. When you are cleaning your room, stay with your breath, keep your mind on your action, and be fully present. As you become more mindful in every way, you will find that you are calmer. The chatter of your mind slows down. And then you will become aware that there is another voice inside you guiding you. As you follow this inner voice, you become your most authentic self, truer, stronger, and truly connected with all that is.

Love you, Satvika. And don't worry about me. I've been traveling for donkey's years now, and this whole world is my home. I've been to a few sites post the fires in the rainforest, and yes, it is definitely not a pleasant sight. I haven't met Dr. Kalamandeen yet, so don't know her personally. But I'm aware of her work. To get a better understanding of the issues on a global scale, you could recommend that your class watches *David Attenborough: A Life On Our Planet.*

And instead of just talking about your experience during the floods, you could present some information about water and the other elements that make up this world as well.

Good luck! I'll tell you more about the global cycles in the next email. Have to go now.

Hugs,
Yogesh

Gateway To Gaia: No.2
Meditation

"To a mind that is still the whole universe surrenders." ~ *Lao Tzu*

1) It is said that all the spiritual wisdom one needs can be found in ancient scriptures like the *Tao Te Ching*. The word "Tao" refers to the flow of life, the way of "being." This is not a religious book, but a way of thinking, a philosophy. It was written by the Chinese philosopher Lao Tzu centuries ago. Here is a poem from it. Meditate on this poem, and see what thoughts it inspires in you.

The Tao abides in non-action,
Yet nothing is left undone.
If kings and lords observed this,
The ten thousand things would develop naturally.
If they still desired to act,
They would return to the simplicity of formless substance.
Without form, there is no desire.
Without desire there is tranquility.
In this way, all things would be at peace.
~ *Tao Te Ching*

2) Try "earthing." Sit on the ground, amidst Nature for some time. How does that make you feel? Be aware of your breathing and bodily sensations as you sit.

3) When speaking to anyone, be mindful of what you say, what feelings your words inspire in others. Do they make others smile? This is speaking meditation. Eat your meals without watching TV or the computer. Be mindful of what you eat, and feel grateful for each bite.

4) Read a good book every day. Reading is also a form of meditation, especially if the book is well-written, uplifting, positive. Reading improves your power of concentration and relaxes you as well.

"I find television very educating. Every time somebody turns on the set, I go into the other room and read a book." ~ *Groucho Marx*

Empty your mind, be formless, shapeless — like water. Now you put water in a cup, it becomes the cup; You put water into a bottle, it becomes the bottle; You put it in a teapot, it becomes the teapot. Water can flow or it can crash. *~ Bruce Lee*

Man is a product of the Earth's surface ... the Earth has mothered him, fed him, set him tasks, directed his thoughts, confronted him with difficulties that have strengthened his body and sharpened his wits, given him his problems of navigation and irrigation, and at the same time whispered hints for their solution ... Man can no more be scientifically studied apart from the ground he tills, or the lands over which he travels, or the seas over which he trades, than polar bear or desert cactus can be understood apart from its habitat. *~ Ellen Churchill Semple*

Since man is not an independent substance, but rather is connected with all elements of nature; he lives off the breeze of air, as well as of the various inhabitants on Earth, food, and drink: he uses fire, absorbing light and contaminating the air: awake and asleep, at rest and in motion he contributes to the alteration of the universe and should he not be changed by that same universe? *~ Johann Gottfried Herder*

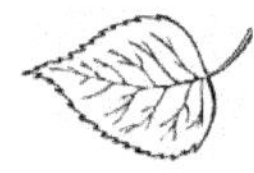

Chapter 3: The Elements

Hi Nana,

Hope all's well with you. Thank you for recommending we watch David Attenborough's movie. The sights he shows us are so beautiful, and the solutions he offers – they make so much sense! Everyone in class loved it. It has made things so clear for all of us. Though I'm still wondering, how does one go about *rewilding* the world besides limiting human population growth and turning vegetarian?

You know Nana, there was a big sigh of relief from all of us in class when we came to that part in the movie about Morocco adopting solar power instead of burning oil and coal! Why don't people everywhere completely quit using coal to generate energy? We've just ended up with soot all over our own faces and futures, haven't we? How ironic! Another thing I found remarkable in the movie was that novel way of farming in the Netherlands! How clever! Makes me believe the climate problem isn't so unbeatable now after all. Good solutions are available, and if we all put our minds to it, surely we will come up with more ways to bring back the glory of Nature and maintain its balance.

Talking of balance, in Earth Hour it was my turn to make a presentation today, on the natural elements, and how important it is to keep them in balance. I spoke first about my first brush with a natural disaster. A number of my friends shared similar experiences to mine about those heavy rainy days of 2015. I said

I was just 5 years old when it happened, but I still remembered those 3–4 whole days without electricity, inverters, cell phones, or screen time, our entire compound and street flooded with dirty water, and the windows rattling constantly under the barrage of the howling winds and rains. Everyone at home had been worried because they couldn't reach you to tell you they were OK, and not to worry about us! Where were you then, Nana? I can't recall now.

I also mentioned to the class how Nicky's house had been filled with water and almost everything inside had been damaged. His family had to be rescued by boat as that part of Chennai had become a lake. While having Nicky for company then turned out to be a good thing – with us playing with shadow puppets in the candle light amidst the torrential downpour – I can't make up my mind yet whether that was the most terrible time we've had so far or the cyclonic storm Vardah that hit us the next year!

Anyway, while digging for reasons for these extremely heavy rains, I came across a study by scientists at the University of Hyderabad and the Indian Institute of Technology Bombay, which states that most likely the heavy rainfall was the result of the rise in surface temperature and the warming of the Bay of Bengal sea. Corresponding it with what we had studied in our science books in school, I explained how that meant since there was greater evaporation of seawater, due to the heat, there had been an increase in condensation or cloud formations, and then the resulting precipitation or rainfall! That's the water cycle, right?

As part of the presentation, I also googled the other elements of Nature, like you suggested. My chemistry book talks about 118 elements, so that was what I was expecting to find. But as per several ancient philosophies, the world is composed of just five elements: Earth, Water, Fire, Air, and Ether (Space). Apparently, all of creation is made up of these five elements in different proportions! Ayurveda says that the Human body is also the product of these 5 elements: 72% Water, 12% Earth, 6% Air, 4% Fire, and the rest, Ether. And when we humans are disconnected from Nature, or adopt ways that go against Nature, this proportion is off, creating our many illnesses. Just as the disproportionate rains create havoc in our lives.

Is this what you meant when you spoke about elements, Nana? Or was there something more?

Much love
Satvika

My dearest Satvi,

During the Chennai monsoons in 2015, I was on an assignment in California Sierra Nevada. The flooding in Chennai, which has been the worst in the last 100 years, happened because the city was not prepared for the huge amount of rainfall. I recall those dark days clearly, and how frantically I had been trying to reach you all then. Terrible times indeed!

When I mentioned elements, I had been referring to the elements that are recycled in Nature and how humanity has been disrupting those processes of Nature, to its own detriment. Your explanation of the water cycle is correct. Similarly, other elements in Nature, too, have their cyclic, self-rejuvenating systems, like the *carbon cycle* and the *nitrogen cycle.*

But the classification of elements you presented stands as most relevant, too. Good job. When we connect with the five elements in Nature, that is Earth, Water, Air, Fire, and Ether, we can restore our health and regain optimum vitality. Each of these elements represents a state of matter in Nature. All that is solid is classified as the "Earth" element. "Water" refers to everything that is liquid. "Air" includes everything that is in gas form, including carbon and oxygen. The part of Nature that transforms one state of matter into another is called "Fire." And "Ether" is the mother of the other elements, as well as the basis of higher spiritual experiences.

Each of these elements is associated with certain qualities. Such as earth teaches us about patience, stability, and dependability. I've already mentioned "earthing." Walking barefoot on the ground also increases the earth element in our bodies, making us calmer, more grounded, and stronger. When there is an imbalance, and the influence of this element is more on our bodies, we feel heavy, sluggish, dull. As Sadhguru Jaggadish Vasudev says, "Whenever you eat food, you swallow a part of the Earth. Essentially, we take in a part of the planet to sustain the body. Consequently, how we treat the planet is how we treat our own bodies."

Similarly, spending more time in the sunlight, we increase the element of heat, or *agni* (fire), and the transformative power in our bodies. This helps us digest better and sleep better, and also gives us vitamin D3, which makes our bones stronger. But what happens when there is excess heat in our bodies? Exactly what happens when someone is always angry or obsessed about something! Irrational thoughts that lead to unwanted consequences.

What about air? Not only the quality of air that we breathe in but also how deeply we breathe in plays a very vital role in keeping us healthy. Places where the air is pure and unpolluted are therefore most beneficial for us, we feel more active, light. And this is also why meditation becomes important, as it leads us to breathe very deeply, which then changes other subtle things in our body, like its frequency, its energy.

The importance of ether, or space, is felt most when we find ourselves in a constricted place, like an elevator, which we can hardly wait to get out of, right? On the other hand, vast expanses, like beaches, forests, farmlands, churches with high ceilings, etc. allow our spirits to soar, giving us a sense of grandeur and joy. Ether is everywhere. It is the space in which the universe exists. In the human body, ether is associated with the empty spaces within our organs, like the lungs, bladders, cells, stomach, etc. When there is too much ether in our bodies, Ayurveda says we feel empty, dissatisfied. Just like when your stomach is empty! With the right nourishment, we keep our bodies balanced, content, and working optimally.

And then there's water. Water is the coolant to our bodies, and being near natural water bodies, like waterfalls, rivers, and oceans, makes us feel calm as well as more energetic. Even dew drops can add to our sense of well-being. Walking barefoot early morning on wet grass is said to be a great source of life force or *prana*, extremely beneficial for health. In our bodies, water is found in all the liquids, like blood, saliva, urine, sweat, etc. When there is insufficient water content in the body, we feel dehydrated, our skin becomes dry, we lose weight, and feel weak.

Our body is a self-rejuvenating, self-healing system that operates best within the laws of Nature. For instance, when the stomach is empty, the baby instinctively cries out for food. Eating the right foods in a timely manner helps us all function properly. When we are tired, we need to rest. The stresses and strains of the day are released and balance is restored when we sleep at night.

The same way, the Earth, too, is a large, single organism, of which we are a tiny part, like a cell is in our body. The Earth, too, is a self-rejuvenating system that self-sustains, and self-heals. It has its cycles, of action and inaction, just as we do.

But what happens to your body when you deprive it of its regular rhythm of action and rest? How do you feel when you go two nights sleepless? That's what we have been doing to the Earth, wittingly or unwittingly. In pursuit of profits, of wanting more and more of progress, humanity has been disregarding the laws of life, its cycles and its rhythms, and the well-being of other life forms that share this planet with us. We have disrupted the order of Nature, and unless we respect that order and work with it, we cannot ensure a green future for our children.

We've sacrificed our better judgments, our intuition, to chase money. We have become unbalanced inside, and that is what we have created outside, by taking this planet and its resources for granted.

To restore the lost balance, life, Gaia, is asking us to back off, slow down, and start giving back for a change, instead of taking all the time. For instance, we say we need trees, for paper, for furniture, and so many other things. Are we planting as many trees as we are cutting down? Are we refilling the cup that we sip from?

It's like how our own banks work, or our relationships. No one can keep withdrawing money from their bank accounts without also regularly depositing money in them. Likewise, you would never accept it if your friends were continuously rude to you yet expected you to smile and be loving to them all the time.

Do you understand now, Satvi? This is why each one of us needs to reconnect with Nature. It is up to each one of us to ensure that we reestablish our strained relations with Mother Earth, with *Darthi Ma*. We have to find that balance within first, for it to be reflected without. To get in tune with the rhythm of life, stop obstructing its processes, and clogging the system with our trash, greed, impatience, and selfishness!

Like David Attenborough sums up in his movie, "Nature is our biggest ally and our greatest inspiration. We just have to do what Nature has done. It worked out the secret of life long ago. In this world, a species can only thrive when everything around it thrives, too."

Hugs,
Yogesh

Gateway To Gaia: No.3
Restoring Balance

"Water is the elixir of life, water contains medicines!" ~ *Atharva Veda*

1) When you wake up each morning, drink 3 to 4 glasses of water, on an empty stomach.

2) Drink a lot of water throughout the day. Do so mindfully, slowly sipping the water, being aware of how it feels coursing down inside your throat.

3) Have a bath at least two times a day. Do so mindfully, imagining that the water cleanses away not just the sweat and grim, but also any negative thoughts and emotions.

4) Try saying affirmations often, even when having a bath, like "I am healed and healthy." "I am clean and pure." "I am water." "I am one with Nature." Positive affirmations make us stronger.

5) Water a plant or plants regularly. If nothing else, you can at least get one pot, with a fresh, new plant, and water that every day. Observe how that grows and changes.

6) Go for a swim often, in a pool or even in the ocean.

7) Spend some time on the beach or near a water body, in mindful meditation. Note how that makes you feel.

"As muddy water is best cleared by leaving it alone, it could be argued that those who sit quietly and do nothing are making one of the best possible contributions to a world in turmoil." ~ *Alan W. Watts*

Your diet is a bank account. Good food choices are good investments. ~ *Bethenny Frankel*

There are people in the world so hungry that God cannot appear to them except in the form of bread. ~ *Mahatma Gandhi*

Healthy citizens are the greatest asset any country can have. ~ *Winston Churchill*

Chapter 4: Food

Hi Nana,

How's Japan? Did you spot the Tanchõzuru there? Apparently, that species of cranes symbolizes a long life and is believed to live for a 1000 years! We saw a lot of cranes here last week when we went on our school trip to the Vedanthangal Bird Sanctuary. Mama said you've taken her several times there when she was a child. It was lovely to see all those birds, but I wish the place was a little better maintained, you know, to make it more tourist-friendly.

Anyways, we had a rather somber, thought-provoking presentation today, in Earth Hour. Sushmita showed us images in stark contrast, of people in several countries around the world starving even today, with all our advanced technology, while in other parts horrible amounts of food are being wasted away! On the one hand, over 800 million people go hungry every day, and on the other hand, on average about 30%, or about one-third, of the world's food is thrown in the trash every day! In the US alone, over 40 million tons are wasted every year! How come we have such a disparity? If there is excess food in countries like America, why aren't we sharing it with the places where people have nothing? Just like how, when we have more food at home after a get-together, Mama shares some with the aunty downstairs, or sends some to the watchman next door. Or how when we go to a restaurant for a meal and there are leftovers, she gets it packed and gives it away to some needy person on the road.

Sushmita showed us a list of some of the worst-faring countries as per something called the Global Hunger Index (GHI). The

GHI is calculated for each country based on the number of people who are undernourished, the number of children below the age of 5 who are underweight, and the number of children below the age of five that die. How sad is that! The higher the score, the worse the hunger problem. While the US and other developed countries don't figure in the list, for obvious reasons, 116 other countries are mentioned. Some countries, like China, Chile, and Brazil, have GHI scores less than 5, which is not so bad. India, I was surprised to see, has a score of 27.5! But several countries, including Congo, Haiti, Zambia, Yemen, Madagascar, Burundi, and Chad (never even heard of some of them before!), have GHI scores in the 30s and 40s. Somalia was at the bottom of the list, the world's hungriest country, with a score of 50! I just can't imagine what kind of life that would be, Nana! To live day in and day out with hunger, lack, and nothing. We really are blessed to have so much choice here. Nani keeps saying, "every time you eat, give thanks for the food." I can see why now!

The saddest were those pictures of little children almost naked, all skin and bones, literally, looking all dirty and lost, with tears running down their faces. Malnutrition is a way of life in a number of these underdeveloped countries, and has been so for years together, with everyone barely getting 1 or 2 meals a day. Really Nana, how come no one talks about these things more?

Sometimes I think just like children love to escape into the worlds of movies or books, adults all over the world especially some leaders, who we assume would be busy being responsible and keeping things in order, love to escape from the real issues by distracting themselves and others with really insignificant stuff! Like renaming roads and building statues! Does the world have any "Leader" at all? How come no one is going to the rescue of these poor countries to help them get on their feet, be happy and healthy, like us? Is there no solution for those helpless, hungry children?

And what came as a shock to us most was that instead of assisting these countries in rebuilding, the so-called "developed" countries, like the US, Britain, and Germany, are dumping their waste on them! Recently, the international police, that is, the Interpol, has estimated that one out or every three cargo containers that leaves Europe carries toxic waste, like old mobile phones, computers, machine parts, TVs, refrigerators, etc., which are them discarded in landfills in some of the poor African and Asian countries, polluting the soil there. What audacity! Instead of coming to their aid, the disadvantaged are being put in graver trouble! Does no one question these successful countries – with their overfed populations – on such inhumane actions? Why? Doesn't anyone see that it is wrong? Is economic development all that the rich countries care about? What about moral and ethical development?

You are right Nana, we human beings have got to fix ourselves on the inside first. Get our perspectives straight, and our values in place, before we can see a better world outside.

Feeling very blue now. I want to get myself a bar of chocolate from our fridge to help me cheer up. Then I think of those little ones in Burundi, millions of them, dealing with hunger every single day of their lives! Shameful and sacrilegious, don't you think? It's like the world is presently full of human beings but hardly any humanity!

Take care, Nana.
Satvika

My dear Satvika,

Hold on to those feelings of angst and dismay. But don't let them get you down. We cannot be of much use to ourselves or others when we lose the will to live well and stand up against the injustices we see around us. Or for that matter when we ignore things and train ourselves to look the other way! Remember the lessons you are learning now, and journal your thoughts in your diary. One day you can put all this knowledge and awareness to good use. Atta girl!

Yes, there are a lot of discrepancies between the "haves" and the "have nots" of this world, even in terms of something as basic as food. One of the main reasons for that is the harsh climatic conditions and geography of most of those poor countries. Other important reasons include a lack of good governance, infrastructure, and education. And it's not like others have never considered passing on the excess food available in one country to those countries in dire need. Doing that, however, would involve a complex logistical operation, which is going to cost someone a lot of money to set up. Though the world community, especially the United Nations, is contributing financial, medical, and other support, to help rebuild those nations, the solution cannot be as simplistic as giving away food for free, year on year, forever. Not even when it comes to the rich giving away to the poor in their own country. There's an old Chinese proverb that sums it up well, "Give a man a fish and you feed him for a day, teach him to fish, and you feed him forever."

That's what the leaders in the world who care enough − and there are many of them − are working toward. In 2015, the United Nations announced a set of goals they call the Sustainable Development Goals (SDGs). These goals are to be targeted by all countries throughout, to create the world we all want, a world with (a) no poverty, (b) zero hunger, (c) good health and well-being, (d) quality education, (e) gender equality, (f) clean water and sanitation, (g) affordable and clean energy, (h) decent work and economic growth, (i) industry, innovation, and infrastructure, (j) reduced inequalities, (k) sustainable cities and communities, (l) responsible consumption and production, (m) climate action (n) life below water, (o) life on land, (p) peace, justice, and strong institutions, and (q) partnerships for goals.

As more and more people are becoming aware, solutions beneficial to all are being sought. But, as I mentioned before, collective effort is called for. Each of us has to ask ourselves this question, "What am I doing to heal our planet?"

Currently, the rising temperatures are creating more complex issues for us to consider. The shifting of seasons is leading to plants sprouting and turning green sooner than usual, and as time goes this causes the plants to become less nutritious, impacting food security everywhere. So, though today we may seem better off than a number of countries in Africa, if human activities continue stoking the fires of the climate problem, if temperatures keep increasing at the present rate, with the air and water everywhere being polluted every day, there's no guarantee that in the future India, or even the US, will not become another Burundi!

Ways and means have to be found to *live sustainably*, which means without using up or destroying our natural resources completely. We have to learn to honor the laws and limitations of Nature, its processes, and work with them. For instance, let's talk about the carbon cycle. I'm sure you've read about *photosynthesis* in school, about how plants absorb carbon dioxide and release oxygen? Plants take in carbon dioxide present in the atmosphere to make food with the help of sunlight. Some of this carbon seeps into the soil below, to be released into the atmosphere again via *decomposition*, which is the rotting of *organic* things like dying leaves. This is the carbon cycle. Some of the decomposing materials way deep underground convert to *fossil fuels*, that's how coal is formed. Human beings have been digging up and burning coal to generate electricity to power our cities and industries for over a hundred years now. We have been adding too much carbon and related harmful agents into the atmosphere than can be safely recycled back into the Earth, via photosynthesis and other natural processes. This has resulted in the increased temperatures everywhere and other domino-like climate changes, leading right back to us, and upsetting our lives as well!

Fixing this imbalance we have set off in Nature requires that we first find our way back to Gaia, and her good graces. We have to address the core issue. We have to heal ourselves, to shift our internal compass from "progress at all costs" to "living in harmony with Nature," before we can see a healed world around us.

You know, Satvi, ironically, there's a concept in Africa called Ubuntu. It means each person is a reflection, and a consequence, of his surroundings, both socially and environmentally. So traditionally, each person there accepts his community as an extension of himself. And when a person strives for happiness, for progress, they only consider themselves to be truly successful and happy when the others in the community are successful and happy, too.

That is what Gaia wants for all that is a part of her, human, bird, or bacteria! The well-being of all. That is the perspective each of us needs to adopt when making our decisions and choices. Because everything plays an equally important role in this Earth system. When we are self-centered, focusing only our happiness and well-being at the cost of that of others, we cannot have long-lasting happiness or success. That just is not possible. Scientifically speaking! One way or another, our actions will bring back to us equivalent fruits. That is what we in India call the Law of Karma. I'm sure you can figure out what's in store for the great waste dumpers around the world!

So go ahead, focus your efforts on your actions. Eat that chocolate, and then get some healthier food to eat. The more fruits and vegetables in your diet, and the lighter your food, the greater your connection with Mother Earth.

The tanchos are doing good. They have been recently brought back from the brink of *extinction* by the timely action of a group of Japanese farmers who took it upon themselves to feed some of these cranes in the winter months when food is scarce. More organizations have joined the effort since, and these cranes are beginning to thrive again.

Love,
Yogesh.

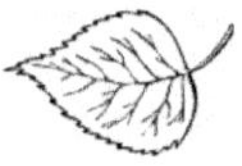

Gateway to Gaia: No: 4
Eating Consciously

There is a common saying, "You are what you eat." So always choose your food wisely.

"Leave your drugs in the chemist's pot if you can heal the patient with food." ~ *Hippocrates*

1) Include more fresh fruits and vegetables in your diet. And avoid non-vegetarian and oily food.

2) See your food as a sacred form of nourishment, a gift from Mother Earth. Develop the habit of eating mindfully, with awareness. Focus all your senses on what you're eating. What does the food smell like? How does it taste? How does it feel in your hands or your mouth? The more aware you are, the more attention you pay to things around you, the more in touch you are with the universe, with Gaia. Distracting yourself by watching TV while you eat is thus counterproductive!

3) Be grateful for each bite, and imagine the nutrients making you healthier and stronger.

4) Eat smaller meals. Eating more than our body really needs makes us feel lethargic and heavy. In the long run, it can lead to other health problems as well, like obesity.

5) Avoid wasting food. When you do get the opportunity, share some with the needy.

"If you truly get in touch with a piece of carrot, you get in touch with the soil, the rain, the sunshine. You get in touch with Mother Earth and eating in such a way, you feel in touch with true life, your roots, and that is meditation. If we chew every morsel of our food in that way we become grateful and when you are grateful, you are happy." ~ *Thich Nhat Hanh*

Being surrounded by nature and animals always kept me grounded and happy. ~ *Alison Eastwood*

Culture is a symbolic veil with which we hide our animal nature from ourselves ... and other animals. ~ *Mokokoma Mokhonoana*

When humanity serves Nature, Nature serves humanity. When we serve animals and plants, they too serve us in return. ~ *Mata Amritanandamayi*

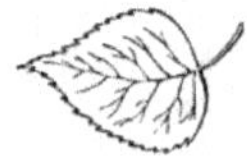

Chapter 5: Animals

Hi Nana,

Something unusual happened here today. Do you remember the stray dog that "adopted" our compound two years ago? Initially, everyone in the building had tried shooing it away because it always looks grimy and unkempt, but it kept coming back. Papa had even called the Blue Cross once and then the Chennai Corporation to come and take it away. The Blue Cross informed us at the time that they were filled to capacity! The Corporation guys came and took it away, but after a few days the dog was back again! Soon someone gave it a name, "Raja," and it became a fixture on our veranda that we began to largely ignore. Then one day the dog gave birth to a litter in our garden! With confirmation now that "it" was really a "she," someone renamed her "Ruby."

In the next few months, we saw Ruby's litter, or what was left of it after she had eaten a couple of them, grow up and wander away. But Ruby remained. Usually, she keeps to herself, walking out to the street whenever she pleases, wandering back again to settle herself in her corner, barely eating anything that's offered to her. She sleeps almost the whole day! But when any strangers approach, she becomes alert and starts barking.

Today, Nani said the dog did something unusual. Nani had gotten into her car for some grocery shopping. The dog came near the car and started whimpering! Nani said the dog looked at her very sadly, and suddenly Nani sensed it was signaling to her that it wasn't safe for her to go out! So Nani got out of the car and didn't go out at all. She said dogs have a sixth sense about things, and for some strange reason this dog, though we just ignore its presence since it anyway refuses to eat anything we offer, had come to care for us.

Pretty amazing, right? Why do you think Ruby did that?

So much for the strange behavior of animals! How do you explain this − I just came across this post on Instagram − a Mexican mayor recently married a 7-year-old alligator who had been dressed up as a bride! Seriously! Apparently, it's an age-old tradition of the indigenous tribal communities there, like a prayer, pleading for Nature's bounty! There was even a picture of him kissing the bride! Weird or what!

Anyway, next week it's my turn to make a presentation again. And I would like to learn and share more about animals and our connection with them. I liked that story about those cranes being brought back from near extinction in Japan! How lovely! I want to talk about more such happenings.

In previous presentations, it's been mentioned that the Earth is currently in the middle of a *Sixth Mass Extinction*. They said the previous mass extinction was the one that made the dinosaurs extinct, and that during all mass extinction occurrences, a majority of the species die, never to be seen again. That's good, when one talks about dinosaurs, sure, but I would hate to see so many other lovely creatures, like butterflies, become extinct!

It is believed that about 500 species of land animals are on the brink of extinction as I'm writing this. Scientists have said that this spate of extinctions underway is the most serious threat to the survival of our own species as well, as we need the others to balance things out in Nature. If they don't survive, neither will we.

Why do mass extinctions occur, Nana? What can be done to save *endangered animals*? And how can we children contribute toward this? Is there no way to bring back or revive a species once they become extinct. Can't scientists find ways to do so? Like in the movie *Jurassic Park*? Is that possible in real life, you think?

Anyway, the Diwali holidays are coming up. Hope to see you then. It will not be as fun without you! Mama asks if you can get some cabbage pickle from there, *Hakusai no sokuseki zuke* (what a mouthful!)

Love,
Satvika

Dearest Satvika,

As long as we are alive, anything is possible. Recently, scientists at the Japanese University of Yamanashi created mice by a technology called cloning, using freeze-dried skin cells. Other animals have also been brought to life via scientific means, but with mixed results. Research is still underway. This climate story is far from over, or our fate sealed. New solutions are sought, and they will be found, I am sure better than we ever expected − provided that the goal and the intentions are for the highest good of all. Once that piece of the puzzle locks in place, once that shift has occurred in the consciousness of every man, woman, and child alive, miracles are bound to follow. We may very well find ways to revive entire species of all kinds, in safe and beneficial ways.

All the loss that is being recorded today, this sixth extinction as they're calling it, is the result of thoughtlessness and lack of awareness among a large section of people who are totally disconnected from Nature. But, every day more and more people are drawn to stand up to this challenge, to share their concerns, and to spread awareness. Because no one wants this to continue. That's why environmental education is being given to children as well, that's why more people are writing books and blogs about it, talking about it, even joining movements and organizations to participate in rallies and demonstrations.

Mankind, and that means every single one of us, needs to begin respecting the fact that nothing in Nature is "extra" or "unimportant." Every single organism, big or small, every bird, animal, insect, germ, and amoeba has a part to play in this system. And if their numbers are reduced drastically, by hunting, pollution, deforestation, etc., imbalance occurs, creating other consequences.

The previous five mass extinctions that occurred on this planet over its 4-plus-billion-years history were due to various reasons, all "natural." Such as drastic fall in temperatures, volcanic eruptions, depletion of ocean oxygen, excess heating or global warming, and collision with asteroids. In each event, 75 to 90% of species populations, sometimes 100%, were decimated. And after each event, the planet took millions of years to regenerate itself. Scientists believe this present mass extinction has been set off by human activities, that it is largely man-made, and is happening at a faster rate than it would otherwise have occurred in the natural course of events.

It is believed that only 2% of species that ever lived are alive today, and even their numbers are reducing every day. This does not bode well for us humans. As Professor Paul Ehrlich of

Stanford University stated, "When humanity exterminates other creatures, it is sawing off the limb on which it is sitting, destroying working parts of our own life-support system. The conservation of endangered species should be elevated to a global emergency for governments and institutions, equal to the climate disruption to which it is linked."

Of course, things are being done to try and salvage the situation, both by governments and independent agencies. But that is not enough. Unless the root of the problem is addressed, unless people like you and me, and that aunty who lives downstairs from you, learn to reconnect with Nature deeply, learn to feel for it genuinely, this will continue to be a losing battle.

Unless each one of us relearns what our ancestors lived by — a deep respect for the forces around us, for the universal spirit that surrounds us and exists in everything — we will keep making bad decisions, decisions that are nothing short of self-annihilation in disguise!

The universal spirit, or life force, or Gaia, whatever we choose to name it, most definitely also resides in all animals. The native, tribal peoples everywhere and across time have recognized this.

The many Native American tribes, for one, saw mankind as being the caretakers of this world. They revered all life forms, seeing them as a larger brotherhood. Animals were seen as sacred beings, as guardian spirits. Each animal had certain qualities they believed, and communicated messages from the spirit.

For instance, the humming bird was associated with healing, integrity, and beauty. It was considered as a messenger of rain, and as a sign of good luck. The wolf was associated with courage, loyalty, direction, endurance, and intelligence. The deer was considered a symbol of intuition, sensitivity, and fertility. The eagle was a symbol of power and courage, and only one who had proved to be courageous could wear a head-dress of eagle feathers.

The Native Americans, like the indigenous people in other places as well, believed that when you see a particular animal, especially repeatedly, Spirit is trying to convey some message. Even when these animals are seen in dreams, or visions. That's why they have also been called power animals or *spirit animals.*

It may well be that the birds and animals we see today carry specific messages for us from the universe. The animals have not changed, remember? We humans have.

We have lost a lot by severing our sacred connection with Nature, and the wild. But it's not late yet. Nature is always supporting us, the Great Spirit is always talking to us.

When we make the effort to be still, we can hear our inner voice, and sense what the animal and plant kingdoms have to share with us.

And yes, perhaps your "stray pet" Ruby is also a spirit animal. She definitely seems to be bonded to your house or someone there. The dog spirit animal is said to bring the qualities of loyalty, love, and steadiness to a person.

But a lot of this knowledge is so subtle, Satvika, that it cannot be understood clearly until it is experienced personally! First let's learn to love and take care of all creatures around us. As we evolve, becoming more true to ourselves, and more aware, more will be revealed to us. All in due course.

As for the Mexican you mentioned, Mayor Victor Hugo Sosa, was just following an age-old tradition. He is from one of those rare ancient, indigenous tribes that still survive. Alligators are seen as symbols of good luck and abundance there, and the wedding ritual was a symbolic invitation for prosperity and plenty from the universe for his community.

Take care, little one. I will be seeing you all during Diwali.

Hugs
Yogesh

Gateway To Gaia: No.5
Caring for Animals

"Animals form an inalienable fragment of nature, and if we hasten the disappearance of even one species, we diminish our world and our place in it." ~ *James A. Michener*

1) What birds and animals can you see from your home? Find out about those that are common to your area, and provide food and water for them. For instance, if you have a terrace visited often by crows, pigeons, and even squirrels, make food grains and clean water in a container available for them every morning.

2) Do you know which birds and animals in your locality are endangered? Lists are readily available now in a number of places on the Internet. Find out more, and if you can, contribute in any way to help them.

3) Don't buy or consume any products made by killing or harming other species, like corals, ivory, leather, tortoise shell, and meat. Encourage others to follow suit.

4) Avoid using plastics, especially *microplastics*, those tiny pieces of plastic that can never be destroyed, *reused*, or *recycled*. Plastics are *non-biodegradable*, which means, unlike dried leaves that decompose and transform into other materials, plastics will remain as they are forever. Which means, for instance, that even when we're gone, all the toothbrushes we've ever used will continue to exist somewhere here on Earth! Unless we stop producing things from plastics, they will keep being consumed by clueless animals, fish, and birds, and end up killing them. What's more, the chemicals from different plastics,

even from dumped clothing materials such as polyester, nylon, polyamide, and acrylic, leech into the soil and nearby water sources, polluting them both. This makes our agricultural produce toxic as well!

The goal of life is to make your heartbeat match the beat of the universe, to match your nature with Nature. ~ *Joseph Campbell*

Your real self, the real you, is everything there is… but concentrated and expressing itself at the point called your physical organism. ~ *Alan W. Watts*

I took a walk in the woods and came out taller than the trees. ~ *Henry David Thoreau*

Chapter 6: Trees

Dear Nana,

Hope all's well with you. Missing our evening walks together! And the 20 Questions Game! I have a few good ones for when you come next time :)

Earth Hour was extra special this week. Each of the classes had to put up a play about the environment for the whole school. It was the turn of Class XI today. And they'd done such a great job! It was about the Tree Hugging Movement, also called the Chipko ("to hug" or "to stick to") Movement.

I was telling Mama about it earlier, and she told me you had been there just after it first happened to take photographs. How was it all? The play was quite exciting, full of drama like a Bollywood movie! Was it like that in reality?

The story goes that way back in the 1960s and early 1970s, a lot of deforestation had been underway in the Himalayan region. And it was all approved by the government. Licenses were given out for the mass felling of trees for commercial purposes. But when landslides occurred in 1970, due to the loss of the trees, the nearby river Alaknanda was obstructed, leading to flooding in the region. Several villagers lost their lives, livestock were carried away, even roads and bridges were damaged.
The local people of the region then realized that their survival depended on that of the trees, that their surroundings were much more precious than any money that could be paid for destroying

them. So, *en masse* the villagers went to the government, requesting them to ban commercial forestry. However, the government officials, in all their ignorance, refused.

So, the logging contractors came back again to cut down more trees. This time though, to ensure they would not be disturbed, they had the men of the village nearby sent away elsewhere on false pretexts. As they approached the forest, the loggers were surprised to find that the women of the village had turned up to stop them now! When requesting, pleading, and cajoling with the contractor did not help, unheedful of the verbal abuse and shouting that were hurled at them, the village women tied sacred thread around the trees and then hugged the trees to protect them. They stayed that way − relieved in turns by the men who had returned − until the contractor finally backed off, which was after 4 days!

When the government learned of this, an inquiry was held, and soon a law was passed making commercial forestry illegal! Hurrah!

Our class presented its play on Monday. Our topic was pollution. And we put up little skits to show how mankind has been polluting air, water, and soil, and how our ingenuity in creating solutions for our needs has become our own enemy. Our vehicles, factories, even our agricultural processes have all been releasing toxins, making our "home" a large crematorium!

Finally, we showed that the pollution of the air, water, and soil are all interconnected, and they all had to be cleaned up to make this planet a safe and healthy place again.

It was a good play, everyone clapped. But the *Chipko Andolan* was way better! What a lovely story! I wish more people would stand up like this and actively do something about our planet, instead of looking at it all like it's a boring movie and not their own story unfolding before their eyes!

Love you, Nana. Take care.

Satvika.

My dear Satvi,

I distinctly recall that visit to the Himalayan region, now called Uttaranchal, in late 1973. The Gandhian Sundarlal Bahuguna had been involved in the Chipko Movement. "Ecology is the permanent economy," he said. And how right the times are proving him!

Unfortunately, the movement is not active anymore. It drew a lot of global attention then, and is still talked about, but it hasn't really stopped deforestation anywhere. Every hour hundreds of trees are still being cut down across the world. For agriculture, housing, industries, further urbanization, and other commercial purposes. A lot of people think Nature's bounty has been placed there for their personal pleasure and profiteering! To pillage and plunder whimsically. They just don't see the invaluable services trees provide for us, and the precious roles only trees can play.

Trees as well as plants are very important for our planet. They are the oldest life forms on Earth, making up over 80% of the global *biomass*. Sure, they provide millions with nourishment. We get our wood, paper, herbs, and medicines from them. But those are just a few of their many "benefits." Trees hold the soil in place, preventing soil erosion and landslides. They help in *carbon sequestration*, that is, the process of absorbing carbon from the atmosphere and converting it into other, more harmless to us, forms. They produce oxygen and release it into the atmosphere. Trees are home to millions of animals, insects, and birds who depend on them for their survival. They add beauty to our urban surroundings and provide shade and privacy. Trees reduce air pollution and heat, and reduce the gases in the atmosphere that would otherwise cause the *greenhouse effect* on our planet. That is, keeping the harmful radiations from the sun, as well as the excess of carbon and methane released by human action, trapped in our atmosphere. And wood from trees has served as the oldest source of *biomass* energy, that is, energy from organic matter, including crops and animal waste.

But, more than that, all trees have a certain energy, a sense of timelessness and stability, that add to our sense of well-being when we are around them. Like animals, trees and plants, too, are alive with spirit. They have a life force, a soul. They are not inanimate, they are not "things," as we in the modern times believe.

Our ancient forefathers were well aware of this. Our sages in India, the Red Indians of America or the Native Americans, the Chinese, the Mayans, the Celtics — across the globe people had the consciousness of spirit dwelling in all things. For ten thousands of years humanity has lived in peaceful interdependence with the natural world around. The indigenous tribes who survive to this modern day continue to live with this awareness and respect for all things in Nature, showing us that it can and should still be the way to coexist. They all share a deep respect for trees, seeking their permission before taking anything from them, and warning them ahead if they had to cut or damage them in any way. Instead of considering such people obsolete, remnants to be borne with, or tolerated, we would do well to listen to what the indigenous folks have to say. A deeper understanding and appreciation is required. For they are the links to a past that has successfully lived in harmony with Nature. And we can learn a lot from them.

Spending time near trees, walking or sitting near them, observing them closely, and contemplating them can bring us fresh insights, even a shift in consciousness. You will find yourself marveling at their ancient beauty, the splendor, and the wisdom they willingly seem to share. How else do you think ancient people recognized the medicinal value of different plants and trees? Like animals, trees too speak, to those who know how to listen.

The ancient people, people of the Earth in the truest sense, believed that each tree has its own fairy, or tree spirit, taking care of it. And that different trees have different qualities, different gifts for us. For instance, while the hazel tree is said to help with creativity, the fir is believed to give one far-sightedness and prosperity, bamboo is said to bring fortune, and oak, wisdom. Each tree has its own magical gifts. Which brings to my mind now that scene from the first movie in the *Harry Potter* series, where they talk about how wands made from different trees have different powers!

Just like all else in Nature!

There is magic to be found all around us, Satvika, in every leaf, in every stream, in every seashell. There is so much to know, to love, and to connect with out there.

So, go hug a tree today! Find your greater family!

Love,
Yogesh

Gateway To Gaia: No.6
Trees

"Adopt the pace of nature, her secret is patience." ~ *Ralph Waldo Emerson*

1) Trees are hundreds of years old. And they have a lot of wisdom to share. Find an old tree (the taller it is, and the wider it is, the older it is said to be), any tree for that matter. Reach out your hand and touch it. Touch its bark, its leaves, its branches. How does that make you feel?

2) Stand or sit with your back to the tree. Take slow, deep breaths, relax, and meditate if possible. You may find yourself coming up with fresh insights. Note them down in your diary. Do you keep a diary? Do so. That is a great way to connect with yourself!

3) Observe a tree and its surroundings. Look at its roots, and the soil beneath. Do this often, with more trees, to become familiar with them.

4) Hug a tree. Really. For as long as you can. Note how it makes you feel.

5) What trees do you see in your garden? Or around your home? Get to know the trees around you better.

It makes no difference as to the name of the God, since love is the real God of all the world. ~ *Apache (Native American) Proverb*

And into the forest, I go to lose my mind and find my soul." ~ *John Muir*

Study nature, love nature, stay close to nature. It will never fail you. ~ *Frank Lloyd Wright*

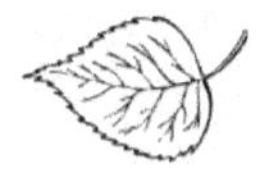

Chapter 7: Love

Hi Nana,

A very Happy New Year to you! I'm so sorry you had to cancel your plans at the last minute. The family get-together was lovely, and we all missed you. Anisha aunty surprised us all with her MJ dance moves! I never knew she could dance! The memory of it still makes me smile :)

For my next presentation this month, for Earth Hour, I have been reading up on the subject of changing coastlines and the sea level rise. Do you have any suggestions for me on that topic? Any related human interest stories that I could share? I love those the best!

Did you know NASA uses satellites to monitor sea level rise? They've even been using supercomputers and other means to investigate the causes of changing sea levels for decades now. And all the while I thought they just send people and rockets into space!

NASA has stated that global sea levels are rising by 30% more each year than when they started monitoring in the 1990s. And most of this has been because of the rise in global temperature. The glaciers in the Arctic have been melting. Analysts believe that at this rate, by 2050 the Arctic will have no snow at all during summers! Other ice caps over Antarctica and Greenland are also said to be melting. By 2100, as a result, the oceans across the world, which together hold 97% of all of Earth's water, are estimated to rise further by 1–8 m. The average depth currently is 3800 m. To put that in perspective, our swimming pools just have a depth of 1.2 m!

As a result of the rising sea levels, coastlines are changing, and the ocean is swallowing up more of the land. This is leading to catastrophic effects on coastal communities, destroying homes and people's livelihoods. Some countries are coping with the changes better than others. For instance, one-quarter of the Netherlands is already below sea level. The encroaching sea is a challenge the country has been dealing with for centuries now. It has invented some creative ways to adapt to and redirect this constant danger to serve safer purposes, like building and maintaining its coastal defenses. One of its innovations, called the Delta Works, consists of a series of dams and storm surge barriers that blocks the ocean from coming into the land. Have you seen it, Nana? The American Society Of Civil Engineers has called this structure one of the Seven Wonders Of The Modern World!

Another point I found interesting is that the Dutch teach their children to swim with shoes and clothes on, just in case there is any sudden flooding. Did you know this? The deeper we get into the subject of climate change, the more insurmountable it seems, and yet when we read such stories, hope dawns again. Still, I don't think a lot of people appreciate what's at stake. Sometimes I feel that we're all characters in a tragedy and don't even know it!

You know, Nana, Mama says our thoughts are very powerful. She says if we hold a vision long enough, it can manifest. Like, when I'm unwell, she tells me to imagine I'm in a pink bubble, and that I'm healed and healthy. If I imagine the Earth is in a huge pink bubble, and repeat every night, "The Earth is green and healed," wouldn't that help?

Love,
Satvika

My dearest Satvika,

Your mother is right. Our thoughts are indeed very powerful, even the thought that "I am not powerful"! The "system", that is, this civilized world we live in, with our daily timetables, schedules, deadlines, our many "authorities" – our parents, teachers, elders, and bosses – thrives on this illusion of powerlessness. We need to respect these, especially our elders, yes, but this has to be balanced with the knowledge that we, too, in our rights are the children of this universe, born with inner wisdom. Often, we give away our power and say it's all destiny! But the truth is, we are always empowered by spirit, just as anything or anyone else. And with the right intentions, we can heal not only our bodies but also this planet. For that, first, we must all connect with Nature with our hearts.

Satvi, have you seen or heard of any bird, animal, or tree comparing itself with others in its neighborhood? They don't, because they are perfect as they are, created by this wonderful universe. Why do humans insist on comparing themselves with others? Mother Earth loves all her children unconditionally. Each one of us here plays an important part that is unique to us. As Robin Sharma, the popular life coach, often asserts, "There are no extras in life." Then where is the question of feeling unworthy or unequal to others? Or feeling that we can make no difference? That we cannot be the "leaders" we seek?

We are all souls here with individual, specific lessons that we have come to learn. So, whether one is rich, poor, beautiful, ordinary, silent, eloquent, enterprising, timid, kind, or cruel, we all matter. Equally. This is one of the core beliefs that we as a society need to work on together. We need to teach our children that they are perfect as they are, no better, no less, than anyone else. We need to teach our children to love themselves, and we need to start loving ourselves more, too. Because love is the greatest force. When we know how to love ourselves, we will know how to love others. When we know how to respect and love our elders, we will know what it means to love and respect the preciousness of life in all its entirety. It all begins with what's happening inside us.

What is it that makes the Dutch come up with engineering marvels that keep their communities safe? What is it that makes the Japanese farmers provide food for birds like the tanchos that are simply passing by? What is it that inspired the village folk of Reni to hug trees and save them from being felled? And what is that one thing that makes this whole world possible?

That power is Love. And we are, each of us, capable of using it for the most magical results.

Today, most of us have become so bound to our technology, that we feel helpless without it. We feel nothing for this planet, for Nature, except for those few rare occasions when something catches our attention as we're passing by to go somewhere else. The modern world is in a hurry, going fast nowhere!

The earlier indigenous shamans and elders of the world had warned about the current state of the world. They had foreseen that while safe in our concrete cages, we were creating illusions of separateness from the rest of the natural world that would one day make us strangers in our own home and a great threat to all of life. But no one wanted to listen to the indigenous folk then.

Ironically, now it is technology that is helping the voices of these indigenous people reach us. And certain cultures, like the Mayans, who still have their shamans and elders, who are still connected to Gaia just as our ancestors were, are taking the opportunity to make the rest of the world more aware of our missteps. And to remind us of what we have lost.

If you Google for them, you will find a number of videos on the Internet where you can listen to their appeals, their stories, as well as their wonderful music. Their pace is slow, and a lot of their time is spent alone, amidst Nature. They say everything speaks to them, this Earth, water, fire, the wind. And they say Mother Earth is crying, calling out to her children, to heal her, to love her creations equally.

Tata Viento, a shaman elder from Guatemala, says, "There is a constant conversation going on beneath the Earth. The roots are in conversation; the roots are all holding hands. But as human beings, we are totally disconnected from Mother Earth. This means we come up very short in how much we care, in how much respect we have regarding human life."

The shamans across the world all know that the way forward is the path of peace, love, and wisdom. That is the basis on which we need to redesign this planet and our place on it. What is required, therefore, is a whole new paradigm of humanity. Nothing else will do.

Love is the basis of all that is good. When we focus on loving ourselves, we allow wonderful events and things to unfold. Because that is what we attract with our loving thoughts. When children are well-loved, they learn to love themselves, and likewise to allow all good things and people to be drawn to them. Isn't that such a simple way to ensure children grow up to be successful and good human beings? Isn't that why my dear Satvika is so full of love for everything and everyone all the time?

You know Satvi, when I was in Lago de Atitalán, in Guatemala, a few years ago, I had the opportunity to spend some time with Tata Pedro Cruz, a Mayan elder. Like others, he believed that love, respect, and gratitude are among the keys to a peaceful and harmonious existence. He said that we must have "Gratitude for everything. This is the trunk of life, the stem of life." Even when someone hurts us or causes harm in any way, one must feel gratitude … for the knock one has received, "for the lessons one has learned. And then we leave no room for conflict."

As for your question, little one, "If I imagine the Earth is in a huge pink bubble, and repeat every night, 'The Earth is green and healed,' wouldn't that help?", yes my dear, of course it will.

For, as the Chaos theory asserts, "When a butterfly flaps its wings in the Amazonian rainforest, it can change the weather half a world away."

We are all interconnected with each other and everything else in Nature. So, keep doing what you can. Keep loving and believing. Spend as much time in Nature every day as you can, and love her more. For she is you.

Love,
Yogesh

Gateway To Gaia: No.7
Love All

"When you look out of your eyes, at nature happening out there, you're looking at you. That's the real you. The you that goes on of itself." ~ *Alan W. Watts*

1) Spend more time in Nature, and make a list of 100 things you absolutely love about it.

2) Do you have a pet? Try to get one if possible. It can be anything, a dog, a cat, a tortoise, some birds, even fish. Take care of it.

3) Spend some time in Nature and create something, like a drawing, a painting, or a poem, inspired by it.

4) Find and read books on Nature — non-fiction or fiction.

5) Go for a picnic with friends and family. See how many different birds and animals you can spot.

6) Whenever you happen to look at yourself in a mirror, tell yourself, "I love you." How does that make you feel?

"There is no problem so big or so small that it cannot be solved with love." ~ *Louis Hay*

Do not be led by others, awaken your own mind, amass your own experience, and decide for yourself your own path. ~ *Atharva Veda*

Don't judge each day by the harvest you reap but by the seeds you plant. ~ *Robert Louis Stevenson*

Everything in nature invites us constantly to be what we are. ~ *Gretel Ehrlich*

Chapter 8: Living Your Purpose

Hi Nana,

It was Career Day in school today, for the seniors. Tamara, my friend from the tenth standard, was telling me about it. Counselors were talking to students first in groups, then they had one-on-one sessions, to discuss about interests, hobbies, and strengths.

Did you know students even have the option to become farmers! Apparently, a young Indian couple quit their hi-tech jobs in the US a few years ago to take up farming here. They live in a town a few hours outside Chennai now, with their two kids who are being home-schooled. What a radical U-turn! The counselors also told Class X that there is a whole new range of job profiles related to the environment, called green-collared jobs, opening up now. Like environmental engineer, urban grower, recycling and waste manager, conservation scientist, sustainability manager, environmental lawyer, limnologist, oceanographer, wildlife biologist, sustainability analyst, water waste management expert, solar designer, urban environment impact officer, environment database administrator, and water resources engineer. Whew! And these are besides the other more commonly known careers like landscape architect, photographer, veterinarian, geologist, etc. The counselors helped the students find the best fits based on their interests, and helped mark out career paths they could focus on.

Papa said they didn't have such thorough guidance when he was in school, and luckily he hadn't needed that kind of help because even as a child he was very clear that he would be an architect one day. Is that how you decided to be a wildlife photographer, Nana? Because that was what you loved to do?

Tamara said that by the end of it she was still a bit confused as to what to choose. So the counselor has asked her to take some time to decide. They have a few months before choosing their high school streams.

When I asked Nicky, he said since he loves watching movies, he is going to be a filmmaker. But Anisha aunty is not happy with that. She says he should choose something more stable and "secure," like engineering or an MBA. She says that is what gets high-paying jobs. "Look at Sundar Pichai," she said. "Look at Tom Cruise!" Nicky retorted.

What do you suggest I opt for when it's my turn, Nana? I love books. So Mama says I could focus on that and become a writer. Go with your strengths, with what you love to do, she says, and you'll do well enough. More importantly, she says, "You will be in tune with your soul, and so working with life, not against it." Deep! I wonder where she gets that from! :)

This reminds me of that lovely movie, *3 Idiots,* starring Aamir Khan. Do what you love to do, because you will do that well, and so are bound to be successful, Rancho says in the movie. Still, how can one be sure to choose what's the best option?

For instance, saying "be a writer" is one thing. But how do I decide what to write about? Does one need a formal college education to be a writer? Or is it just enough to get started with the basic knowledge of the language? Like, say, right now, as a child author? And, if I do choose to write, should I write about the environment because it is in a critical condition now? Maybe that could be my contribution to saving the environment? I like the sound of that!

My last presentation for Earth Hour is scheduled next month. Then we have our final exams. The year seems to have gone by so swiftly! Hope to see you soon!

Love,
Satvika

My dear Satvika,

Every decision you make, especially the ones with long-term consequences, like choosing a career or a life partner, is best taken from the inside out. Aligned with your soul, and in tune with life. Yes, Mama knows best, indeed!

So, what does it mean to be "aligned with one's soul"? How does one know for sure? If one is in touch with one's intuition, one's inner voice, such confusion would never arise. Only when someone is disconnected from himself, unsure of what he feels about anything, or feels obliged to smother his own inclinations to please others that conflict arises within a person, and with that come uncertainty and lack of clarity.

"I pay no attention to anybody's praise or blame. I simply follow my own feelings," said the great musician Wolfgang Amadeus Mozart. That is a person looking at the world from the inside out. In touch with his feelings, and deeply connected with his intuition. From that state, anything created is fluid, almost spontaneous, and the musician becomes a mere channel of life itself!

When everyone is encouraged to follow their intuition, to respect their feelings instead of being imposed upon, or made to follow "trends," then each person will be in the flow of life, living his or her specific purpose, playing the role only they can play. Like the cells of the human body. They may look more or less the same, but each does the work assigned to it, so that the organism works efficiently!

Now imagine, we are each a cell of this great organism we call Planet Earth. If each one of us stays in our own lane, following the guidance of our soul, this planet will be a healthy, happy one. When we are deeply connected with Nature, when we spend more time "being," whether it is outdoors or meditating indoors, or writing in our journal, we are automatically connected with ourselves. We then make authentic choices, based on what we are led to do from within.

I chose to be a wildlife photographer because I've always loved Nature. Back when I was a child, our city had a lot more greenery. I used to visit Adyar and the barely touched surrounding areas along the river there often, taking photos with the Kodak 35, my very first camera, my father had gifted me. The decision to make that passion a life-long vocation was an easy one!

The world around us now is one where a number of people base their decisions not on their heart, on how they feel, but on their head, their egos, by rationalizing to themselves. The "cognitive dissonance" within us thus is being reflected without. As Earl Nightingale puts it, "What happens inside always appears outside."

So, if humanity, and that includes every single one of us, wants to see a healthier planet, we must heal ourselves first. We must relearn what it means to be "one" with Nature, aligned with all of life. We must begin following our hearts, and our intuition. Live authentic lives, following the guidance given by life constantly. When we do that, when we listen, really, we will find the way, to the right career, and a better planet.

From that awakened state of consciousness, all our decisions will automatically be good ones, bearing bountiful harvest for all concerned. We will be living our purpose, and so will be in harmony with the universe. Rich or poor, black or white, we would each be in service of others, with humility, knowing we are all playing out roles assigned by our souls and life itself.

Hugs,
Yogesh

Gateway To Gaia: No.8
Living Your Purpose

"Your purpose in life is to find your purpose and give your whole heart and soul to it." ~ *The Buddha*

1) Accept and acknowledge all your feelings. They matter.

2) Spend time alone with yourself often, especially when you need to make any important decision. Check in with yourself before asking anyone else for their advice.

As the Native Americans believed, "Our first teacher is our own heart".

3) Pay attention to things around you. When you look at a flower, really look at it. Make being mindful your habit. This keeps you grounded, and balanced.

4) Trust yourself and your inner voice. Politely stand up for yourself, because no one knows you better than yourself.

5) Be true to your purpose and the decisions you are led to make from within. Be consistent always.

6) Don't let any fears stop you. Understand them and work around them. Focus on the love, and let it be your power.

There is no last word in research, and that includes climate research. It's never the truth that scientists offer, but only our best possible approximation of reality. But that often gets forgotten in the way the public perceives and describes our work. ~ *Hans von Storch*

We live in a world we ourselves create. ~ *Johann Gottfried Herder*

If you really think the environment is less important than the economy, try holding your breath while you count your money. ~ *Guy R. McPherson*

Chapter 9: Awakened Choices

Hi Nana,

How's Indonesia? The pics you WhatsApped to Mama look absolutely wonderful! Those tarsiers remind me of Kreature from the *Harry Potter* series! And what are those giant flowers called? So beautiful! I remember seeing a sculpture of one in the Singapore Zoo three years ago.

Anyway, I had a fantastic presentation on *solar energy* today. Thanks to Papa, I was able to take my class for a site visit to the green office building that's on the road parallel to our home. We saw how the solar panels on the roof are used to power the offices below, effectively reducing the environmental impact of the building by a good 30%. The Facilities Manager then explained other aspects of the building that helped make it more environment-friendly. To conserve water, dual plumbing was used throughout the building to recycle water in toilet flushing. The building itself has been constructed with recycled stone and metal. Windows have been placed effectively so that more natural light can be made available, and to reduce electric lights for the better part of the day. To promote indoor air quality, materials that emit no or low toxicity have been used.

Nana, did you know that many commonly used materials in our homes, like wall paints and upholstery, give off harmful gases that affect the health of the residents? Green buildings are constructed and designed in such a way that only the safest of materials are used for the health and well-being of all inhabitants, as well as the surroundings.

But my question is, why aren't people warned that certain materials are hazardous? Just like it's done on cigarette cases, why isn't there a warning on air fresheners, floor cleaning agents, and even some curtain materials that they release harmful gases? Most people are unaware that their homes and offices are not as safe as they assume! If the manufacturers are aware, why do they continue to make such stuff available? Why don't they do the necessary research to produce better things, so that every building is a green one?

Papa says it because of the force of habit! We're used to a certain way of doing and being, and unless we're pushed, we don't make changes easily! Albeit, currently India is the world's third largest producer of renewable energy, generated from an assortment of sources including solar power, wind, small hydro, big hydro, bio-power, and even nuclear power. Together they help generate more than one-third (38%) of the electricity we use. For the balance (62%), we are still burning up fossil fuel!

Like other countries in the world, India has made a commitment, by signing the Paris Agreement, to reduce this to 50% by 2030. That is a move the government is making. But what about the common folk? Papa has added some panels to our terrace, but as of now they serve only as a supplementary source of power. Why don't more people switch to using solar power at home on their own accord, without waiting for it to become a law or trend? Like plastics. For years people have been saying plastics are not good for the environment, but unless they were forced to, unless the use of plastics was officially banned, most continued to use them. And some still do!

What is it going to take for humanity to fully wake up from its deep slumber? To rise to the occasion, and consciously choose how it lives, day in and day out?

Love,
Satvika

Dearest Satvika,

Do you know who it was that first tried to harness solar power? One of the giants of the Renaissance Era, Leonardo da Vinci, way back in the 15th Century. Recognized as one of the world's greatest artists, da Vinci was also a reputed polymath, a draftsman, an engineer, a scientist, a sculptor, a theorist, and an architect, with a number of innovations to his credit. And, what makes this all the more interesting is that he was largely self-taught! A man who lived by his heart, following wherever his curiosity, his intuition, led him.

Leonardo required no university degree to validate him. He never sought the world's approval. He just remained deeply, silently, joyously in tune with himself, with his inner calling of the moment, exploring, discovering, and inventing this world. The man just did what he "had" to do, what he was constantly being led to do by his curiosity and intuition. He was true to himself. And that was enough! That accomplished a lot.

His prodigious output, in various forms, like paintings, drawings, machines, buildings, and writing, had people calling da Vinci a genius. Where do you think he got his insights from? The same place you get yours from, when you are still, and listening to that inner voice.

"I have from an early age abjured the use of meat," said da Vinci, "and the time will come when men such as I will look upon the murder of animals as they now look upon the murder of men." Like all the wise people who ever lived, da Vinci also believed that "everything connects to everything else."

Everybody wants to be successful, rich, comfortable, and happy. And we all deserve to be. Progress is good, yes, but it is worth nothing when it goes against the laws of Nature, against the way or the flow of life. Only when we realize this, when we begin making choices that our soul approves of, only then can we be truly happy in every way.

When we begin making more awakened choices in every aspect of our lives, we will be ensuring not only our well-being but that of everyone and everything around us. For instance, when you have to buy an air conditioner, find out which one in the market is the most eco-friendly. When you buy a light bulb, check if it is energy efficient. Seek out more information and make informed decisions, led by your heart, not just by the price. And when you learn about the harmful effects of a product, say an air freshener, inform the manufacturer or supplier about it. Ask them to replace it with a safer product. Spread the word to friends and family to avoid using questionable items. Report it in the local paper. And if you can put your mind to it, invent a better product yourself! Why not? The choice is always ours.

Dealing with our waste, especially our electronic or e-waste, is another area which requires our discretion. This is where our lack of balance, our thoughtlessness, is most striking. There's no arena we've left uncluttered with our rubbish! Right from our streets, to our rivers and oceans, and far out into space, human waste is splattered wherever any one of us has ever been. This is because we have so far been focused only on what we get out of things, not how the rest of the world is impacted by our actions.

Take Indonesia, for example. A beautiful country by all accounts, no doubt. It is, in fact, one of my favorite places in the world. Its bountiful variety of flora and fauna is barely matched by any other country. That large flower you were asking about is the *Rafflesia arnoldii*, the world's largest flower, and perhaps the stinkiest, found only in Indonesia. The forest covers here are thick, with a never-ending supply of breathtaking subjects to capture on camera.

Indonesia is a country made up of over 17,000 islands, but only about 6000 of them are inhabited, with people living largely along the coastlines. It is the fourth most populous country. And the third worst emitter of greenhouse gases! It is also an important exporter of fossil fuels.

In the past several years, activities like deforestation and forest fires have contributed much to global warming, a direct result of which is the rising sea levels and lost coastal areas witnessed by the country. Today, the people of Indonesia are being asked by the world community to choose differently, to conserve its forests and plant new ones, and to use its rich resources wisely. But most Indonesians refuse to believe that climate change is a real problem and that they are actively contributing to it! This is despite the many natural disasters that have been striking this island nation in the recent past, including earthquakes, droughts, floods, fires, storms, and tsunamis.

Denying there is a problem, pretending it is not a problem, and anesthetizing ourselves with food, TV, and other forms of entertainment are not going to make the problems go away. They are choices as well, and obviously not awakened ones. Educating ourselves and correcting our ways, therefore, is imperative, so that going forward we can make wiser choices.

In the end, Nature will triumph. She will reclaim what is hers, but let's not forget, we are a part of Nature, too. We are Gaia's own, and she is guiding all of us, she always has been. We just need to start listening again. The universe has our back, always, and humanity will rise to become its own savior, and the savior of this planet, inspired by Gaia! A lot of changes are underway, but the problem we've created is far bigger. As more of us realign with Nature, learn to be still and mindful, as we transform to be our authentic selves and reconnect with our hearts, all will be well once more. So don't be disheartened. Just do your bit. That is what we each are required to do. Just our bit. That will be enough. You'll see.

Hugs,
Yogesh

Gateway To Gaia: No.9
Awakened Choices

"The only way to make sense out of change is to plunge into it, move with it, and join the dance." *~ Alan W. Watts*

1) Whenever possible, especially when traveling short distances, avoid vehicles that burn up fuel. Choose to walk, or go cycling instead.

2) Join a carpool if possible for places you "must" go by car.

3) Reuse, recycle, and reduce whatever you can.

4) Planes burn up a lot of fossil fuels to stay up in the air. Avoid using planes as much as possible. Next time opt for a train journey!

5) Avoid unnecessary purchases. Buy only what you need. Remember the adage, "Simple living, high thinking."

6) If you must own a vehicle, opt for an electric one.

7) Start using more renewable forms of energy. Find out options available to you, such as solar power at home.

8) Cut down on meat and dairy products.

9) Use your resources wisely. As they say, "Waste not, want not." Turn all switches off when not using a room.

10) Share your learning about making awakened choices with your friends and family.

Native American Tribe Navajo's Chants (translated)

I have been to the end of the Earth.
I have been to the end of the waters.
I have been to the end of the sky.
I have been to the end of the mountains.
I have found none that are not my friends.

The Earth is beautiful
Its feet, they are beautiful
Its legs, they are beautiful
Its body, it is beautiful
Its chest, it is beautiful
Its breath, it is beautiful
Its head-feather, it is beautiful
The Earth is beautiful.

I see the Earth.
I am looking at her and smile because she makes me joyful.
And the Earth is also looking back at me and smiling.
May I walk joyfully and lightly upon Her.

May there be joy.
May there be success.
May there be good health.
May there be well being.

The mountains—I become part of it.
The flowers, the evergreen tree—I become part of it.
The morning moisture, the clouds, the bodies of water—I
become part of it
The wilderness, the water drops, the pollen—I become part of
it.

Chapter 10: Oneness

Hi Nana,

Summer vacations are here! A whole stretch of 55 days with absolutely no schedules! No summer classes of any kind! No keyboard, no badminton, no Tamil tuition! I've even taken a break from coding for the next two months! Isn't that awesome!? I feel refreshed simply thinking about it! Believe me, it was a hard-won battle. Mama finally agreed, on the condition that if she ever heard me say even once that "I'm bored," or if she found me watching more than my quota of screen time for the day, the deal would be off! Don't worry, that's not going to happen!

Nicky, Sushmita, and I have solid plans for the holidays! We've made a list of parks in the city, and will be visiting them all, one by one. We'll cycle to a park early each morning, to avoid the traffic, and will head back mid-afternoon, before the maddening peak hour rush. We're filling our backpacks with lots of goodies, like good books to read, sketch books, our journals, cameras, some tasty food, and plenty of water! We're also carrying our own trash bags. We're going to walk around each park leisurely, visiting it again another day if we like it enough. And if possible, we hope to pitch in with some cleaning, gardening, or watering the plants there.

Nicky's planning to capture our trips on video, and post them on his YouTube channel, hoping to inspire more children to spend time out and about in Nature! Perhaps some of them will join us. It all sounds great right now, and I hope it turns out much better than expected! I'm so excited! :)

I have one more great news for you! Papa's making arrangements for a vacation to Manas Wildlife Sanctuary in Assam. He said once he receives confirmation that we can visit, he'll call you to join us. Do come, Nana, please, please! I just know for sure it'll be a totally different experience with you there! Have you been there before?

Papa says it's the most spectacular of all wildlife areas in India, with a rich variety of plants, trees, and animals. A "biodiversity hot-spot" he called it. It's part of the Manas Tiger Reserve and provides habitats for some rare and endangered species as well, including the tiger, one-horned rhino, swamp deer, pygmy hogs, roofed turtle, hispid hare, golden langur, and the Bengal florican. What a variety!

The sanctuary covers a vast area with various natural landscapes, like a range of forested hills, alluvial grasslands, and tropical evergreen forests. With the majestic Manas River flowing through it! It will be great fun exploring. I can hardly wait!

You know, Nana, Tamara's parents wanted to go to the US for a holiday, like they do almost every summer vacation, to meet their family there. This year she refused to go. She said unless there was a real valid reason to do so, she did not want to step inside a plane ever again! Because planes give off so much of those greenhouse gases! Isn't she a hero! Her parents finally gave in, and this year they're going to Kerala instead, by road!

Reminds me of that old, old proverb, "Little drops of water make the mighty ocean."

Or as that grand old man, Lao Tzu, reminds us, "A journey of a thousand miles begins with one step." BTW, I've been reading your copy of the *Tao Te Ching*. Loving it totally!

Take care, Nana. See you soon.

Love,

Satvika

My dearest Satvika,

I'm so glad you're reading Lao Tzu. After Nature, books are our greatest treasures! There's so much wisdom to be gained from reading a good book every day.

Yes, I've been to Manas, a few times. It has been recognized, both nationally by our government and internationally by several natural conservation organizations, as a very important site for its pristine wilderness, and its rich biodiversity. But it is not just India's Project Tiger reserve, it is also considered a biosphere reserve, an elephant reserve, and an important bird area. As a matter of fact, it was declared to be a World Heritage Site, by UNESCO in 1985.

About 500 species of birds have been found living here, nearly 60 mammal species, 42 reptile species, and 7 amphibians. The wild buffalo population here is believed to be the only pure strain of this species found anywhere in India. As for the rich variety of plants and trees, there are over 89 tree species, 49 shrubs, 37 undershrubs, 172 herbs, and 36 climbers recorded, besides the ferns and different types of grasses. Together these provide a range of habitats. All made the more beautiful peppered by the variety of wildflowers, including 15 species of orchids.

Manas Wildlife Sanctuary is located at the foot of the Himalayas. On the east, it abuts the Royal Manas National Park of Bhutan. All boundaries of this wildlife preserve are highly protected, and special permission is required to visit and explore it. But this is just one. There are 6 other similar national parks in Assam, and 16 wildlife sanctuaries, which are all highly protected by the Government. What's more, there are over 100 similar reserves spread across India.

After the SDGs were agreed upon in 2015 by the world leaders, more action is being taken. The Indian Government and its officers, notwithstanding the many imperfections, has contributed considerably toward helping reduce global warming. Several public sector enterprises, also known as Navratnas, have been contributing significantly to the *sustainable* growth and development of India. One such company is the NLC India Limited, formerly known as Neyveli Lignite Corporation Limited. Although it is a major fossil fuel mining company, started in the 1950s to generate thermal power, recently, it has diversified into renewable energy production. It has installed a 141 MW solar power plant to generate electricity from photovoltaic cells as well as a 51 MW windmill power plant. It targets generating 4250 MW of renewable energy by 2025. You'll be happy to know, currently India is the third largest producer of energy from renewable sources.

Likewise, the National Building Construction Corporation has implemented a policy to incorporate environment-friendly features into its projects, like zero waste, dual piping, rainwater harvesting, solar energy, smart electricity metering, and LED/energy efficient fixtures. In keeping with the Green Building standards, steel structures, modular construction, pre-cast, pre-fab components, and lightweight concrete slabs are used by the company. It also ensures strict adherence to guidelines to reduce air and water pollution at its project sites.

And it's not just in India, governments in several countries are taking significant steps to work toward possible mitigation of the climate crisis, and to help the people live more wisely, and sustainably. Per recent records, some countries like Albania, Paraguay, and Iceland get all of their energy from renewable sources. And Norway gets nearly 97% of its electricity from hydropower. In *third-world countries,* like Ethiopia, Chad, Haiti, etc., organizations like the UN are helping the local governments to be more proactive in this regard and find their own solutions.

But there is only so much any government or organization can do. Instead of shifting the blame around, hoping for Superman to show up, or a miracle, we need to see what we can do in our capacity as citizens of this world. The onus lies with each one of us walking this Earth.

So, what are we going to do now that we have greater awareness? Are we going to step up, and follow through? Are we going to take the responsibility to do the right thing even when no one is watching?

There's a concept in ancient Indian philosophy, a mantra or affirmation, repeatedly chanted by the sages to themselves, *Tat tvam asi.* It means "I am that." This is the basis of *Advaita* philosophy, which means "without duality," or One. No dichotomies.

This world, and all in it, are ONE. That is what the ancients believed. That is what Sai Baba says, and the Buddha, and anyone who ever mattered.

We are, all of us, deeply interconnected with the world around us. When I go for my walk each day, that is what I feel. Oneness, with all of life. In that moment, I am the Sun above me, the butterfly flitting by, the flower dancing in the wind, the koel making its lilting music, and the squirrel scampering away on a mango tree. I am that. And so much more. This is what the world needs to awaken to, and this is the shift we require now, a deep inner knowing that we are in reality a cohesive whole, one with the rest of this universe. One with Mother Earth.

Then, we will begin to understand more than can ever be explained to us. Like what the wonderful Sufi poet Rumi meant when he said "You are not a drop in the ocean. You are the entire ocean, in a drop." It's time to wake up.

See you soon, Love.

Yogesh

Gateway To Gaia: No. 10
Oneness

"A friend is someone who helps you up when you're down, and if they can't, they lay down beside you and listen." ~ *Winnie the Pooh*

1) Today, whenever you remember to, wherever you are, no matter what you're doing or looking at, say silently to yourself, "I am that." Repeat it as many times as you can.

2) Take some time to be alone, indoors or out. Be mindful of your thoughts, your presence, your "beingness." Then when you feel very calm, centered, imagine your breath is sending out love to the whole universe. Breathe in "calm," breathe out "love."

3) The next time you find yourself upset with anyone, before you say anything harsh, calm down and count to 10. Then tell yourself mentally, "I am that." Forgive that person, at least mentally. Remember, everyone is always doing their best based on their current level of awareness. If they knew better, they would behave differently.

4) Today, whenever you meet someone, find something to appreciate about them. Then say that aloud to them. How do you think that makes them feel? How does that make you feel?

"Remember who you really are, trust yourself, and open your eyes to the beauty of a new Earth unfolding before you as we breathe." ~ *Hopi (Native American) Proverb*

Further Reading

1. https://earth.org/kids/

2. https://kids.nationalgeographic.com/

3. https://www.sloww.co/tao-te-ching/

4. https://www.unicef.org/environment-and-climate-change

5. https://bengalflorican.org/

6. https://digital.library.upenn.edu/women/zitkala-sa/stories/stories.html

7. https://navajocodetalkers.org/navajo-chants/

8. *Buddha: A Story of Enlightenment*, by Deepak Chopra

9. *Mirror Work: 21 Days To Heal Your Life*, by Louis Hay

10. *My First Summer in the Sierra*, by John Muir

11. *The End of Nature*, by Bill McKibben

12. *The Life of Birds*, by David Attenborough

13. *The Miracle Of Mindfulness: The Classic Guide to Meditation by the World's Most Revered Master,* by Thich Nhat Hanh

14. *Walden,* by Henry David Thoreau

Glossary

Anthropogenic: Caused or influenced directly by human activities, such as the burning of fossil fuels, rather than by such natural processes as respiration and decay.

Biodiversity: The wide variety of plants and animals that co-exist in their natural environments.

Big Bang: The explosion of a small, dense, and hot matter from which this universe originated more than 13 billion years ago.

Biomass: Total amount by weight of life forms existing in an area. It also refers to potential energy from vegetation.

Biodegradable: Capable of being decomposed or transformed by biological means, thereby not creating pollution.

Carbon Cycle: A natural process of transformation of carbon atoms as they move between live forms and the atmosphere in a cyclical manner.

Carbon Sequestration: The absorption of carbon by the plants or the storage of carbon deep underground in reservoirs, preventing build-up of carbon in the atmosphere.

Climate Change: A long-term, sweeping change in global temperatures and weather conditions. Sometimes these are natural. Currently, they are the direct result of human actions.

Decomposition: The natural process of change or decay at the end of the life of an animal, plant, or other life forms, when it disintegrates and transforms.

Deforestation: The extensive felling or burning of a large number of trees leaving large clearings in forest areas. Birds, animals, and other life forms relying on these trees are also affected.

Ecology: The system of interrelationships between organisms and the environment. Also the study of the same.

Environment: All that is around us. The surroundings and all influencing agents.

Endangered Species: Plants or animals that exist in such small numbers that they could soon become extinct.

Extinction: The process of becoming extinct, that is, completely eliminated or destroyed. Never to be seen again.

Fossil Fuel: Any organic material, such as coal or oil, formed by decomposition of other natural matter, and which can be burnt to generate energy. They also result in toxic gases.

Gaia Theory: A hypothesis that asserts that Earth, or Gaia, is a self-regulating organism, of which we are an integral part. The scientists who put forth this theory believe that all life forms "influence their abiotic environment, and that environment in turn influences the biota by Darwinian process".

Greta Thunberg: A young climate activist from Sweden who came into the limelight after her climate strikes in 2018 and her inspirational speeches in the following years.

Greenhouse Effect: An effect known to usually occur in greenhouses, with the heat from the Sun entering the greenhouse via the glass but remaining trapped there with no way to circulate out again. Burning of fossil fuels is said to cause this effect in our atmosphere, raising the global temperature unnaturally.

Hydropower: Also called hydroelectric power, this refers to the generating of electricity by using the force of falling or fast-moving water.

Ice Age: This refers to the Glacial Period, when large parts of the Earth's surface was covered by glaciers due to the very low overall temperatures.

Industrialization: The large-scale development of various industries in a region for economic purposes, usually accompanied by extensive use of electricity, and thus increase in air, water, and soil pollution.

Microplastics: Very tiny pieces of plastics, usually resulting from disintegration of larger plastics. These are non-biodegradable, and so a health hazard for all animals and sea creatures.

Native Americans: Also called the First Americans, these are the indigenous inhabitants of the United States, found largely along the Western side. They lived off the land for over 15,000 years before their continent was "discovered" in the 15th century by Christopher Columbus.

Non-biodegradable: Not capable of being decomposed by natural processes. So they remain as they are forever. In case of waste, especially electronic waste like old computers, this means they remain piling up in landfills with nowhere to go.

Non-renewable: Anything that cannot be restored. In terms of natural resources, this refers to oil, coal, petroleum, etc., which once used up cannot be regenerated.

Nuclear Power: Electricity generated by use of nuclear reactions. This accounts for about 15% of the world's electricity.

Organic Matter: This refers to substances derived from recently living organisms, mainly plants, but also some from animals, like their waste.

Pangea: A supercontinent that assembled around 350 million years ago, and which began drifting apart some 200 years ago. The Earth was not always the way we know it now.

Plastic: This is a generic term that includes all synthetic materials made by man with the help of combinations of various chemicals. They are non-biodegradable and best avoided.

Permafrost: In the extremely cold regions, like the Arctic, the ice that remains frozen permanently, creating a hard ground, is called permafrost. Structures had been built on this hard ice in many places earlier. With the unexpected global warming now, this permafrost has begun to melt, with dire consequences.

Recycling: The process by which waste materials are transformed to make something new out of them, thus giving them a new lease of life.

Renewable: With regards to natural resources, this refers to sources like solar energy, which have the potential to last or be restored endlessly.

Rewilding: The concept of demarcating special areas where the wild animals can be allowed to exist abundantly, thus restoring balance in Nature and in the food chain.

Solar Energy: Electricity generated by the heat from the sun. Compared to use of fossil fuels, this has 0% emissions, but the technology has its own hazards that are still to be ironed out.

Sustainability: This refers to use of environmental resources in such a way as to avoid using them up completely, and maintaining balance in Nature.

Tectonic Plates: These are the separate sections of the Earth's surface on which the seas, continents, and other geological forms rest. Sometimes these plates can brush against each other, causing severe damage to life above.

Wind Energy: This is another form of renewable, clean, and sustainable energy. It is generated by harnessing the force of the wind, using windmills and wind turbines. Environmental impact is minimal.

Appendix

1. Pangea

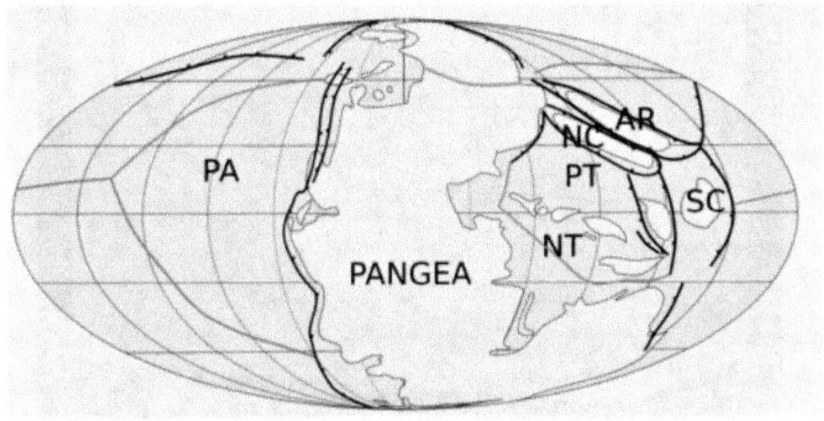

Source: Kent G. Budge, CC0, via Wikimedia Commons

2. Photosynthesis

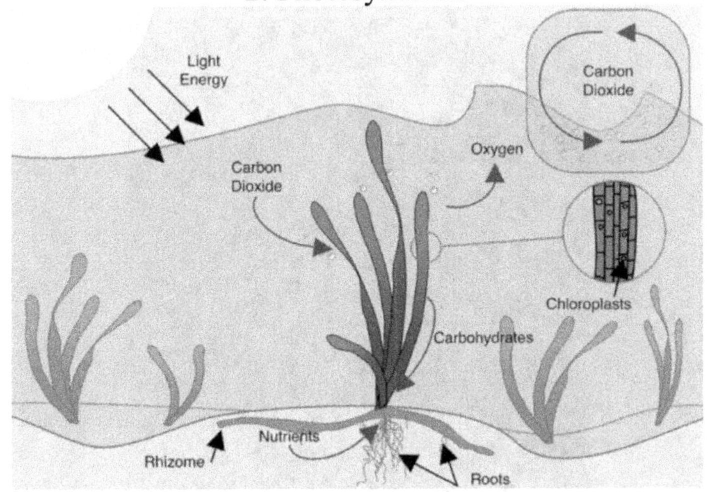

Source: Creative Commons

3. Carbon Cycle

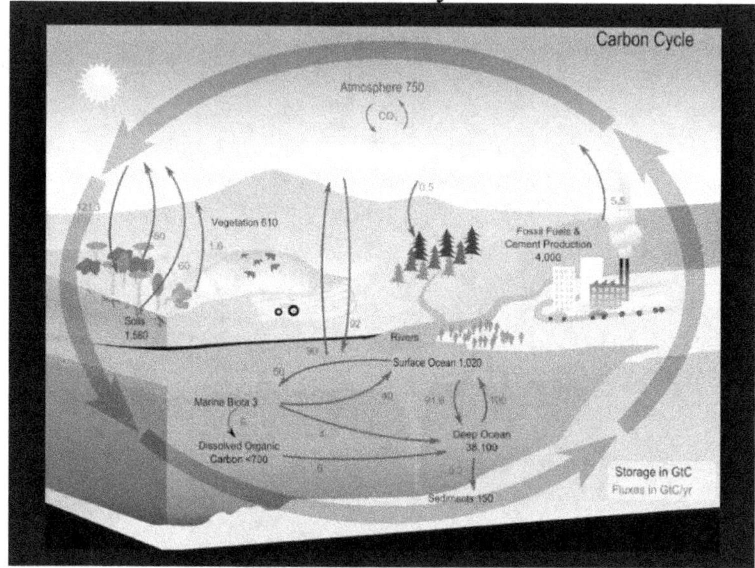

Source: NASA via Wikimedia Commons

4. A Native American

Source: Harris & Ewing, photographers, via Wikimedia Commons

5. Tanchõzuru

Source: Japan National Tourism

6. Dutch Delta Works: Sea Barrier

Source: www.dreamstime.com

7. Chipko Movement

Source: Wikimedia Commons

8. Dead Albatross with plastic inside its body

Source:USFWS via wordpress.org/openverse

About the Author

Dharshana Bajaj is an editor and visual artist. She creates evocative paintings steeped in Nature, and in the sensory exploration of the natural world. Some of her work also reflects her understanding of Advaitha philosophy, which considers that we are all one, interconnected with Nature and each other on a very quantum level.

"As an artist, I believe I can contribute to the awareness of the beauty and glory of the natural world we have been blessed with."

Dharshana believes that when each of us wakes up to the truth that we are not "apart" from Nature, but "a part" of it, we will start making better choices collectively. Her philosophy about mankind's interrelationship with Nature is the basis for this book as well. And as in her art, here too you will find an amalgamation of spirituality, science, and art.

Gaia's Own: Every Child's Guide To Living In Harmony With Nature is Dharshana's first book.

To contact the author/artist, and to see more of her work, do visit www.dharshanabajaj.in.